Legal Almanac Series No. 59

LAW OF ENGAGEMENT AND MARRIAGE

by FRANCES W. KUCHLER, LL.B.

*This legal Almanac has been revised
by the Oceana Editorial Staff*

Irving J. Sloan
General Editor

FOURTH EDITION   SECOND EDITION

1978 Oceana Publications, Inc.
Dobbs Ferry, New York

42184

Library of Congress Cataloging in Publication Data

Kuchler, Frances W.
   Law of engagement and marriage.

   (Legal almanac series; no. 59)
   Bibliography: p.
   Includes index.
   1. Marriage law—United States—Popular works.
2. Betrothal—Law—United States—Popular works.
I. Title.
KF510.Z9K8   1978   346'.73'016   78-3470
ISBN 0-379-11107-1

© Copyright 1978 by Oceana Publications, Inc.

Manufactured in the United States of America

CONTENTS

Chapter I

CREATING THE MARITAL STATUS

Marriage has been defined as the voluntary union of one man and one woman for the duration of a lifetime. Marriage is also considered a contract in that there are certain definite obligations to be performed and rights which accrue to both parties because of the marriage relationship. However, there are certain requirements which must be met before the marriage contract can be entered into as a valid marriage, and these differ in many respects from those necessary to create the usual form of business contract; in fact, marriage is a unique type of contract in that the parties involve their whole personal lives in the relationship.

Marriage is also considered a status, a civil status, and as such is an important part of the legal and social aspects of society, it is to a large extent the foundation of our present society. Because of the vital part that marriage plays in our civilization, the state has always had an interest in its regulation. In our country, the regulation of marriage has been left, by the Federal Constitution, to the various states, although the Federal government has jurisdiction over marriage in the territories. Accordingly, our fifty states have passed their own laws on marriage and some of these may differ considerably from those of the other states.

COMMON LAW MARRIAGE

Before the enactment of statutes there existed the common law of the land. This comon law was inherited by us from England, and some of our states still recognize various of its aspects. Common law was based on precedent and custom, and a whole body of law grew up on this basis concerning the regulation of human affairs.

A part of this law included what is known as common law marriage. In this type of marriage, no license need be obtained and no ceremony is performed. The mutual declaration of a man and a woman to be man and wife and their expressed intent to so remain for the rest of their lives might be considered a marriage, provided that there were no impediments to such a union, such as the fact that one of the parties had a previous spouse to whom he or she was still married, or that one of the parties had a total lack of the mental capacity necessary to understand the significance of the relationship.

There is a division of thought upon whether this type of marriage must be proven by habit and cohabitation or whether the mere establishment of a contract of marriage is sufficient to create a common law marriage. This division stems from the fact that there is disagreement on what constitutes the asumption of the marriage status, whether the statement of the intention of the parties is sufficient or whether there must be a continued holding out to the world by such parties to be husband and wife. The declared intent of the parties must be that both will assume the obligations of a marriage and live together as husband and wife in the same manner as they would had there been a licensed marriage and a formal ceremony. These two schools of thought would only become apparent in the event that the marriage was questioned and had to be legally proved.

Present laws in a number of our states give affirmance to a common law marriage and consider the persons so married to be entitled to all of the rights and subject to all of the responsibilities of a valid marriage. Following is a list of those states which recognize common law marriage, of those which recognize it if entered into before a certain date, and of those which do not recognize it at all.

Common law marriage is recognized in the following states and territories:

2

Table I

COMMON LAW MARRIAGES

States which recognize Common Law Marriages

Alabama	Kansas[1]	Rhode Island
Colorado	Montana	South Carolina
Georgia	Ohio	Texas
Idaho	Oklahoma	District of Columbia
Iowa	Pennsylvania	

*States in which Common Law Marriages are
Recognized Conditionally*

Alaska	(if entered into before 1917)
California	(if entered into before 1895)
Florida	(if entered into before January 1, 1968)
Indiana	(if entered into before January 1, 1958)
Michigan	(if entered into before January 1, 1957)
Minnesota	(if entered into before April 26, 1941)
Missouri	(if entered into before March 31, 1921)
Nebraska	(if entered into before March 31, 1921)
New Jersey	(if entered into before December 1, 1939)
New York	(if entered into before April 29, 1933)
South Dakota	(if entered into before July 1, 1959)

States which do not recognize Common Law Marriage

Arizona	Maryland	Utah
Arkansas	Massachusetts	Vermont
California	Nevada	Virginia
Connecticut	New Hampshire	Washington
Delaware	New Mexico	West Virginia
Hawaii	North Carolina	Wisconsin
Illinois	North Dakota	Wyoming
Kentucky[2]	Oregon	Puerto Rico
Louisiana	Tennessee	

[1] But the parties are subject to punishment for not obtaining a license.

[2] In Kentucky, common law marriages are valid only for the purposes of the Workmen's Compensation Law.

3

No common law marriage results where, by means of a sham marriage, the parties cohabit but do not dwell together as man and wife. Likewise, what has been called a companiate marriage does not create a common law marriage. In this form of association, the parties thereto do live together a husband and wife but the relationship may be ended at the will of either party. Or, there may have been an actual legal marriage but the intent of the parties before the marriage was that it might be dissolved by divorce at any time merely upon the desire to do so without any legal cause for a divorce. Neither is there a common law marriage where the individuals cohabit with the mutual understanding that a marriage will take place at some time in the future.

An exception to the marriage which may be terminated at will is the Indian tribe marriage. By Indian custom these marriages are valid and therefore are so considered by our state laws where the marriage takes place between members of the Indian tribe or between an Indian and a person outside of the tribe. In this instance, the parties must be living according to and being governed by the laws of the tribe. However, in some of our states the marriage laws have been enacted to include Indians, in such cases the Indians must conform to the laws of the state in which they reside.

Suppose that two people are residents of a state such as Alabama or Colorado where common law marriages are recognized and then later take up residence in another state such as Arizona or Arkansas where common law marriages are not recognized. What happens to their marriage in this state?

Do all of the property and support laws apply to them or must they enter into a statutory marriage in the new state of residence? The general rule is that a state will give effect to a marriage which was good in the state in which it was contracted provided, however, that it is not repugnant to the laws of the second state. Usually, a common law marriage will be given the same effect as a statutory mar-

4

riage since it was recognized in the state in which it took place. In later chapters restrictions on marriage will be discussed and it will be seen that there are exceptions to this general rule, such as marriages between persons of different races.

LICENSED MARRIAGE

The usual type of marriage is of course the one which conforms to statutory requirements. Each state has its own requirements as to the age of consent and methods of obtaining the license, as well as restrictions against marriage, such as the prohibition because of blood relationship or racial difference.

Age of Consent

At the common law the age at which a person was considered old enough to consent to a marriage was fourteen for the male and twelve for the female. This is still in use in some states where there must be a marriage of expediency such as caused by the pregancy of the female. Below these ages consent is deemed impossible.

The majority of our states have raised this age by a few years and it is usual that the male must be at least eighteen years of age and the female at least sixteen in order to be able to contract a marriage. These ages are permissible with the consent of the parent or guardian of each party.

Most of the states have lowered the age of matrimonial consent from twenty-one to eighteen years. Whereas, formerly the age of consent differed for males and females, now in most states there is no discrimination between the sexes in this respect. The accompanying table illustrates this point, giving the ages below which a marriage is prohibited and the ages at which the parties may marry without the consent of their parents. As has been previously mentioned, the parties may marry below the prohibited ages where the female is pregnant. Sometimes a court order is required to permit the parties to marry under these circumstances.

5

When a marriage occurs in which one or both of the parties is under age, the marriage may be annuled or it may be ratified by the party under age when he or she reaches the statutory age of consent. This is true only when there are no other impediments to the marriage. Ratification consists in cohabitation with the other spouse voluntarily upon reaching proper age and thereby continuing the marriage relationship.

Mental Capacity

Since the contract of marriage must be consented to by both of the parties about to enter into this status, it is essential that both are mentally aware of the various obligations and legal rights which arise by reason of the marriage contract. Therefore, no person who is insane or an idiot may contract a legal marriage. It has been held, however, that a person whose mental capacity fluctuates from time to time may be validly married provided that he or she was mentally competent to understand the relationship at the time the marriage was entered into. In earlier days, the spiritual side of marriage was stressed more than the legal side, and the mental requirements were not very stringent. At the present time laws provide that one must have sufficient mental capacity to understand what the marriage contract implies and also must have full possession of the power to dispose of his person and property. A marriage which has taken place by the consent of a person who is lacking in mental capacity is one of the grounds for an annulment, which will be discussed in a later chapter.

What constitutes consent to a marriage? There are no specific words which must be spoken to constitute consent to a marriage. It is enough that a marriage is intended and that the parties take up the marriage relationship after expressing their intent to do so.

Neither does parental consent take any specific form. Generally the lack of parental consent is not a cause for annulment, although in some cases it has been held that the parent whose consent was not given may have the right to have the marriage annuled.

Physical Capacity

A party to a marriage must have the physical capacity necessitated by the marriage relationship. This means that there must be no structural physical defect which makes cohabitation impossible and it presently applies to freedom from venereal disease in addition. Most of our states have made it a statutory requirement that the male, or, in some states, both parties, have a serological test within a specified time limit before the marriage takes place and the certificate of a physician stating that the party is free from this form of disease before the license to marry may be obtained. The accompanying table 1 gives the statutory requirement in this regard for each of the fifty states. It will be seen that most of the states now have this prerequisite.

Physical incapacity such as impotence is also a ground for an annulment of a marriage and is included in that portion of the book.

OBTAINING THE MARRIAGE LICENSE

A marriage license may be obtained by application to the officer authorized by state law to issue such licenses. This officer may be a county clerk of the peace, an ordinary or his deputy, a county recorder or county clerk, a clerk of the district court, a recorder of deeds, a probate judge or any other officer so designated by the laws of the particular state in which the parties are to be married. In a majority of the states the license must be obtained in the county in which the parties intend to be married; in some states in the county in which the prospective bride resides.

Either the bride or the groom may apply for the license although in some jurisdictions both must apply in person. In the District of Columbia, for example, a third person may appear on their behalf to give the necessary information. The information required for the application must be given upon oath or affirmation or, where both parties do not appear, by affidavit. It must include the names and ages of the parties and whether or not there has been a previous

7

marriage. If so, the means by which this previous marriage was dissolved must be stated. Some of the states require more detailed information for the application, such as race, names of parents and even the occupation of the male applicant. This is the case in Hawaii. In Virginia also the applicants must state their race or color.

While it may be sufficient to state that there has been a dissolution of a previous marriage, a great many jurisdictions require a certified copy of the divorce decree or certificate.

WAITING PERIODS

Assume now that the prospective husband and wife have passed the physical examination and have presented the medical certificate with their application for a license within the period set by law. A license to marry will now be issued.

Note that the parties are still not married.

The license must be delivered to the person who will perform the ceremony. Many jurisdictions require that the ceremony be performed within a specific period of time after the license has been issued. A ceremony which is performed after this statutory period has expired will be invalid. (See Table II).

Aside from the maximum limitation, some states require MINIMUM WAITING PERIODS. These states insist upon a minimum waiting period between the time that the license to marry has been issued and the ceremony. These provisions are outlined in Table II, in which it should be noted that some states have longer waiting periods for non-residents than for residents.

Many jurisdictions provide for a waiting period between the time that the application for the license is made and the day on which it is issued.

Another waiting period required by some states is that no ceremony may be performed for a stated time after the serological test was made.

Table II also indicates which states have statutory requirements governing MEDICAL CERTIFICATES and WAITING PERIODS.

The above mentioned table may seem complicated at first glance. A review of the provisions in one state may clarify the situation.

In New York, before John can validly marry Jane he must do the following:

1. Obtain a certificate signed by a duly licensed physician, stating that both he and Jane have been given a serological test and found free from infection.
2. Present this certificate within thirty days after the date of the examination along with the application for a license to marry.
3. After receiving a license, deliver it within sixty days to the person who will perform the ceremony. However, in New York, the ceremony may not take place within twenty-four hours after the license has been issued or within three days from the date of the physical examination.

THE CEREMONY

The marriage ceremony may be performed by a minister of the Gospel, a judge or justice of the peace, or by a minister of any organized religious society. In some religions, such as the Quaker faith, where there is no minister, the marriage will be recognized if it has been performed according to the rules and regulations of that society.

Although Delaware, Maryland and Virginia require that there must be a religious ceremony, there is generally no particular form of ceremony required by law provided that the parties consent to the marriage and express their intent to enter into the relationship of husband and wife.

The requirement for witnesses and their number also varies in the different states. Whether or not a marriage has taken place between the parties, if this should become questionable, may be proven by the rules of evidence in the state in which this fact must be decided. These rules of evidence are general for the trial of all types of legal cases.

9

After the ceremony has been performed a certificate so stating must be filled out on the marriage license, which is then sent back to the official who issued the license. He in turn must send the license to the proper recording official. All marriages must be recorded and are usually done so in the office of vital statistics of the county in which the marriage was performed. Copies of the record may be obtained from this office.

If one wishes to inquire as to whether or not a marriage has taken place, it is necessary to search the records in the county in which it was performed. This might become difficult in the event that one does not know which county this was. There is no central recording place for each state. In this area, as in that of divorce, records are sometimes impossible to find since one cannot practically go through the records of each county of every state.

VIOLATION OF STATUTORY PROVISIONS

There are penalties provided by statute against the officer who issues a marriage license unlawfully or against a person who performs a ceremony when he is without authority to do so. The law of Nevada, for example, states that a person who undertakes to join others in marriage, knowing that he is not lawfully authorized to do so or that there is a legal impediment to the marriage, is subject to a fine and imprisonment.

These penalties do not apply to the parties who have been so married. As stated in the Maine statute: a marriage solemnized before a known resident of the state professing to be duly authorized is not invalid because of lack of authority, nor is the marriage invalidated by omission or informality in entering intention of marriage, provided the marriage is in other respects lawful and is consumated with full belief of either party that they are lawfully married.

Table II.

LEGAL AGE FOR MARRIAGE AND LICENSE REQUIREMENTS

State	Minimum Age F	Minimum Age M	Parental Consent Required if Below Age of: F	Parental Consent Required if Below Age of: M	Medical Required for License	Waiting Period Before License	Waiting Period After License
Alabama	14	17	18	21	yes	no	no
Alaska	14	17	18	21	yes	no	no
Alaska	16	18	18	19	yes	yes--3 days	no
Arizona	16	16	18	18	yes	no	no
Arkansas	16	17	18	21	yes	yes--3 days	no
California	16	18	18	21	yes	no	no
Colorado	16	16	18	18	yes	no	no
Connecticut	16	16	18	18	yes	yes--4 days	no
Delaware	16	18	18	18	yes	no	yes*
District of Columbia	16	18	18	21	yes	yes--3 days	no
Florida	16	18	21	21	yes	yes--3 days	no
Georgia	16	18	18	18	yes	yes--3 days	3 days if under age
Hawaii	16	17	18	18	yes	no	no
Idaho	16	16	18	18	yes	no	no
Illinois	16	—	18	18	yes	no	
Indiana	17	17	18	18	yes	yes--3 days	no
Iowa	16	18	18	18	yes	yes--3 days	no

* 24 hours for residents; 96 hours for out-of-state residents

11

Table II. Continued

State	Minimum Age F	Minimum Age M	Parental Consent Required if Below Age of: F	Parental Consent Required if Below Age of: M	Medical Required for License	Waiting Period Before License	Waiting Period After License
Kansas	18	18	18	18	yes	yes--3 days	no
Kentucky	16	18	18	18	yes	yes--3 days	no
Louisiana	16	18	18	18	yes	no	yes--72 hours
Maine	16	16	18	18	yes	yes--5 days	no
Maryland	16	18	18	21	no	yes--48 hours	no
Massachusetts	12	14	18	18	yes	yes--3 days	no
Michigan	16	—	18	18	yes	yes--3 days	no
Minnesota	16	18	18	18	no	yes--5 days	no
Mississippi	15	17	21	21	yes	yes--3 days	no
Missouri	15	15	18	21	yes	yes--3 days	no
Montana	16	18	18	21	yes	yes--5 days	no
Nebraska	16	18	19	19	yes	yes--5 days	no
Nevada	16	18	18	18	no	no	no
New Hampshire	13	14	18	18	yes	yes--5 days	no
New Jersey	16	16	18	18	yes	yes--72 hours	no
New York	14	16	18	21	yes	no	yes--24 hours
New Mexico	16	16	18	18	yes	no	no
North Carolina	16	16	18	18	yes	no	no
North Dakota	15	18	18	18	yes	no	no

State	Minimum Age F	Minimum Age M	Parental Consent Required if Below Age of: F	Parental Consent Required if Below Age of: M	Medical Required for License	Waiting Period Before License	Waiting Period After License
Ohio	16	18	18	18	yes	yes--5 days	no
Oklahoma	15	18	18	21	yes	no	no
Oregon	15	18	18	18	yes	yes--7 days	no
Pennsylvania	16	16	18	18	yes	yes--3 days	no
Puerto Rico	16	18	21	21	yes	no	no
Rhode Island	16	18	18	18	yes	yes--5 days	no
South Carolina	14	16	18	18	no	yes--24 hours	no
South Dakota	16	18	18	18	yes	no	no
Tennessee	16	16	18	18	yes	yes--3 days	no
Texas	16	16	18	18	yes	no	no
Utah	14	16	18	21	yes	no	yes--5 days
Vermont	16	18	18	18	yes	no	no
Virginia	16	18	18	18	yes	no	no
Washington	17	17	18	18	no	yes--3 days	no
West Virginia	16	18	18	18	yes	yes--3 days	no
Wisconsin	16	18	18	18	yes	yes--5 days	no
Wyoming	16	18	21	21	yes	no	no

Chapter II

SUPPORT

The Obligation of Support

It is common knowledge that a man has an obligation to support his wife, as well as his minor children. There are few people who have not heard of the Domestic Relations, or Family Court, wherein proceedings against a negligent husband may result in an order to pay a suitable amount to his wife and children if he has been lax in his duty to provide for them. The procedure in these courts is simple; if complainant wives do not have their own attorneys these will be furnishd by the court.

Desertion: Every state in the United States has a statute applicable to this obligation. The man who deserts his family, without justification, and leaves them in a destitute condition is subject to criminal as well as civil liability. The severity of the sentence varies in different states; fines range from one hundred to one thousand dollars and jail terms may be from one to several years in duration. Desertion, often described as "wilful neglect," is classified by the criminal laws as a misdemeanor or even a felony, a felony being a more serious crime. The MAINE statute defines desertion as a felony if it is of a "high and aggravated" nature and as a misdemeanor when it is not so regarded. The penalty for the felony, for instance, in MAINE is a fine of not more than five hundred dollars and not more than two years in prison, or both. For the misdemeanor it is a fine of not more than three hundred dollars and not more than eleven months in prison or both.

By the usual court procedure, the husband may be permitted to post a bond as a guarantee that he will pay the amount that the court has ordered for the support of his family and thereby escape the criminal penalties. This is naturally a more practical solution to the problem and is therefore much more frequent than actual commitment. The court has many circumstances to consider in the determination of cases of this sort; the extent and availability of the wife's means, their children, and her possible pregnancy are important factors. Some states have statutes which specifically provide for the desertion of a pregnant wife and the penalties which these describe are more severe than for cases of ordinary desertion.

As in the case of all crimes, there are defense to the crime of desertion. A husband may be excused from supporting his wife where she has given him good grounds for divorce according to the laws of the state in which they live, or if she has abandoned him for no justifiable cause. A divorce or a separation agreement whose terms are complied with are other adequate defenses. If the husband can prove his "inability" or inadequacy because of illness or infirmity, he is also excused from the duty of supporting his wife.

From reading the desertion and non-support statutes one might be inclined to assume that, since there were strict laws on the subject, there could not be very many cases in which families of wives and children were left destitute if the husband were employed. As a matter of fact, however, desertion is one of the most serious of our social and economic problems.

Enforcement of Support: The legal means of enforcement is complicated by the fact that it is usually very difficult to serve a summons or warrant of arrest on a man in order to bring him into court. (Even when he is actually before the court he may successfully conceal his assets or earning abilities. In large cities there are so many cases of this sort that there is not sufficient time or means for courts to give each case the attention it deserves.) The greater number of men who desert their families go into other states in order to avoid their responsibilities. Unless a wife is in a fairly advantageous financial position she connot hire a detective or an attorney to assist her with her problem. There are various agencies which are active in this sort of work.

Recently there have been *uniform state support laws* enacted which might prove valuable in reducing the number of families who are public charges because of a deserting parent. These laws make it possible for a dependent wife to state her case to the court of the state in which the husband resides without being personally present.

In order to do this, she must present her case to the family or domestic relations court where she resides. The judge of that court will then forward her verified petition with all of the facts, and will certify that the summons, which has been issued out of his court for the defendant, has been returned with an affidavit to the effect that such defendant could not be located. The judge of the second court (which has jurisdiction over the husband) will then issue a summons out of his court and fix a time and place for a hearing. If the defendant denies the statements in the wife's petition, the proceedings will be halted until both courts have sufficient proof of all of the facts. The complainant wife is represented in the second court by a state's attorney or similar officer. In this way, testimony and evidence are passed back and forth between the courts until a final decision has been reached. The second court, if the husband has been found to be at fault, will then order him to make payments, which will be forwarded to the first court where they will be duly given to the wife.

Today, every state has adopted either the Uniform Support of Dependants Act or Uniform Reciprocal Enforcement of Support Act, amplifying the procedure to compel support of dependents whose responsible relatives are in other states.

These laws are *civil laws* and not criminal laws. There are good social and psychological reasons why it is not considered advantageous to the family relationship to regard a deserting husband as a criminal. (There is an earlier group of uniform desertion laws which were criminal and which applied criminal means to enforce the husband's liability.)

Mutual Obligation: What of the wife's obligation toward her husband for support? The marriage relation, or "status" as it is known legally, imposes a duty on both parties. Sometimes the states deal specifically with this duty and sometime it is included in statutes having broader applications, such as those defining the obligations of various members of the family toward their pauper relatives. CALIFORNIA provides that a wife must support her husband out of her separate property if he is unable to care for himself, or is infirm. (MONTANA and OKLAHOMA have statutes on the subject of marriage obligations which state that both spouses owe each other respect, fidelity and support). The husband must support the wife, but if he is unable to do so she must assist him. NORTH and SOUTH DAKOTA have similar provisions. COLORADO, IOWA and others state that there is a joint liability of husband and wife for the support of the family and that family expenses are chargeable upon the property of both. In these states the spouses can be sued jointly to recover expenses incurred by others.

Extent of the Obligation: There are many people who may be interested in the extent and kind of support which those responsible must give to their families. Is a husband obligated to give over all of his earnings to his wife and children, or is this a matter for his personal determination? The Desertion Statutes say that a man cannot leave his family in necessitious or destitute circumstances, but as a practical matter, just what does this mean? The courts of all of the states generally agree that a husband is liable for

18

his wife's necessaries, and that he is also liable to third persons who supply her with these necessaries when he fails to do so. The same liability applies to those responsible for the care of minor children.

What are "necessaries" to a wife and family must be determined from the circumstance of each particular case, as a court usually finds that the customary mode of living is the yardstick by which the amount of support is measured. However, there are some general rules which have been followed in this matter. "Necessaries" to a family always include: houshold furniture, rent, clothing, groceries, heating, cooking, laundry, education of the children and medical care. Included in the circumstances which excuse a husband from his liabilities toward the support of his wife are her "misconduct," that is, generally, adultery on her part. Some courts hold, nevertheless, that a husband must pay his wife's medical expenses whatever the cause of their living separately may be. Legal expenses are a necessary, sometimes even when the wife is at fault.

There are many instances where a wife has an income from her own separate property, or is carrying on a business which would be adequate to support her and her children. If such a wife can and does contract for her own necessaries, then she is personally liable for them, but if she does not, the husband remains liable even though the wife could afford to pay her own expenses. This duty of the husband is a fundamental one and arises from the marriage relationship itself, although there may be cases in which a valid agreement between husband and wife may allow for modifications of this rule. A husband is liable for his wife's premarital debts only to the extent of property which he acquired from her by reason of the marriage.

It is the general rule in the states in which these acts are effective that divorce does not relieve the father from support of his minor children. However, where the decree awards exclusive custody to the wife, the husband cannot be found guilty of wilful desertion of the child. In those cases where the wife deserts the husband without reasonable cause, he cannot be held liable for her support. Where the separation is a voluntary one, the husband's obligation to support his wife continues. In all cases of support it must be shown that there is ability to support. If the husband is unable to support his wife and minor children, because of illness or inability to find employment, he cannot be convicted under the desertion statutes.

Support of Minor Children

As has been mentioned, it is generally the father who is charged with the support of his minor children. There are criminal statutes in all of the states making it a misdemeanor or felony for a man to neglect his children. These statutes are often a part of the abovementioned laws relating to desertion.

If the child has no father, then the person who has custody over him is considered the parent and has the same duties and obligations which a natural father would have. Support of a minor child means proper physical care and a suitable education for the child according to the financial means of the family and their station in life. Where the father is unable to support the children, the wife must undertake this obligation.

If the child is an illegitimate one whose father has not acknowledged him, his mother is his natural guardian and has sole custody over him. An illegitimate child, according to one definition, is "a person begotten and born out of lawful wedlock." This definition is a clear one where there has been no marriage at all between the parties but it will be remembered from previous chapters that a number of marriages are declared void at a later date. As we have seen, the children of these marriages may be held to be legitimate by the court which has dissolved the so called marriage. Sometimes the legitimacy of such children is dependent upon the circumstances of the marriage and the good faith of one or both parties of the marriage. If both parties, realizing their lack of capacity to contract a valid marriage, nevertheless attempt to do so, the children

20

of this marriage may be declared illegitimate. The children of an incestuous or of a mixed racial marriage are usually illegitimate in those states which have statutes prohibiting such marriages.

Where there has been a valid marriage there is a strong legal presumption that the children of the marriage are legitimate and therefore must be supported by the father. This legal presumption is based upon principles of natural justice. Unless the husband is proven to have been absent for a certain length of time during the period when conception occurs, the wife's children are deemed by the law to be his own. Even in those cases where there is evidence of the wife's adultery and a consequent divorce, there must be additional proof to render her children illegitimate. Where it is obvious that conception has taken place before the marriage, the child is presumed to be the child of the husband and wife.

The support of minor children where there has been a divorce, annulment or other dissolution of the marriage is a matter for the court in each individual case. Support of children after a divorce or separation will be considered in more detail in the book dealing with the laws of divorce and separation in all of the states.

Property Rights of a Wife

At the present time, one is so accustomed to the fact that a wife may hold property as well as her husband that few may realize that this was not always true. A series of laws, which were first enacted in England in the Nineteenth century and more recently in all of our states, known as the "Married Women's Property Acts," first made it possible for a married woman to hold property without her husband's interest and control. Our states, therefore, always have a particular statute defining the "separate property" of a married woman and her rights, interests and liabilities.

MISSOURI, for example, defines the "separate property" of a married woman as: "all the real and personal property belonging to her at the time of the marriage or coming to

21

her during the marriage by gift, bequest or inheritance, or purchase with her separate means or out of her separate labor, together with the income and profits thereof." This is her sole property and under her sole control. MISSISSIPPI states that marriage shall not impose any disabilities on a woman with regard to the ownership and disposition of her property. NEW JERSEY uses broader terms, that is, a married woman's separate property includes property which she receives or obtains in any manner after her marriage. Some states provide for the recording of the wife's separate personal property in the office of the county recorder, so that there will be no possible confusion over her title to it.

Formerly, when husband and wife were considered legally as one person, the husband being "the one," a wife could not make any contracts by herself. This theory is still apparent in five states which do not permit a wife to contract regarding her real estate without her husband's consent. In TEXAS, the signature of the husband is necessary for the conveyance and encumbrance, such as mortgaging, of her own real estate, and is also required for the transfer of her stocks and bonds. In ALABAMA, FLORIDA, INDIANA, NORTH CAROLINA, likewise, a husband must join in his wife's contracts to sell or mortgage her own land.

Generally, the Married Women's Property Acts of all of the states provide that a wife's property shall not be liable for the debts of her husband. There may, however, be some slight modification of this rule, such as the VERMONT law which makes the annual products of the wife's property liable for the debts of the husband which were created because of the purchase of necessaries for his wife and family or for the improvement of her separate real estate. Her property is liable for family expenses only in those states where it is expressly stated that the property of both is charged with the expenses of the family and children. In such cases, the statute usually limits the wife's liability to reasonable and necessary family expenses and education of the children.

Included in a wife's separate property are her earnings. These may be acquired by reason of a regular wage earning position or by means of a business venture. In the latter event the wife may contract solely, without her husband's consent, in her own business matters, even in those states where she may not convey land without his consent. In TEXAS, however, a wife must, with the consent of her husband, petition the court for the purpose of becoming a "femme sole" (single woman) to carry on her own business or trade.

The word "earnings" has been variously interpreted by the courts. That is, money earned inside the home or in connection with a husband's business is often considered as a part of the husband's property and not that which belongs solely to the wife.

If a wife is a wage-earner, she is now entitled to her own damages where such are recovered in an action for personal injuries. If the husband has paid the medical expenses, he may claim reimbursement out of the damage award, in addition to his damages for the loss of her "consortium" (or companionship). There is no such comparable action permitted to the wife. As most of our states now have Workmen's Compensation laws, we may add that a compensation award for injuries to a wife who is employed belongs solely to the wife, and not to her husband.

Community Property

Do our laws define the separate property of a husband as well as that of a wife? In addition to the Married Women's Property Acts there have been other statutory changes which alter the common law rule whereby all property ownership was vested in the husband. There are at present eight so-called "Community Property" states. In these states all property which does not specifically belong to either the husband or the wife is community property which is, in a broad sense, owned by both of them.

Historically, this system did not originate in England as most of our American laws, but was a part of the Civil law of Spain, and was first introduced here in those states whose territory was once in Spanish possession; that is: ARIZONA, CALIFORNIA, LOUISIANA, NEVADA, NEW MEXICO and TEXAS. IDAHO and WASHINGTON copied their earlier statutes on this subject from the CALIFORNIA laws.

All of the community property states make the husband the spouse controlling the common property, but in some states his control is limited. The most important limit is his incapacity to sell or encumber the real estate without his wife's signature (joinder), although generally he may dispose of the personal property without her consent. However, there can be no such conveyance which would defraud the wife of her interest in the community property.

At the death of the husband the wife assumes the role of an equal, since she becomes the owner of her share of the community property, of which half is now under her control. The half which belongs to the husband, if he has not disposed of it by his Will, may go to his descendants, or it may go to the wife. The states vary in this respect.

Neither spouse has testamentary disposition of more than his (or her) half of the common property. If such an attempt is made, the other spouse may elect to take this share against the Will.

Marriage Settlements

As we have seen in a previous chapter, the fundamental duty of a husband to support his wife may be altered by an agreement between the parties. These contracts will be recognized as valid by the courts only if both parties had capacity to understand the nature of the agreement and if the contract was not brought about by undue influence or fraud. They will be set aside if the court finds that they are unfair to either party, or against public policy.

The consideration for such a contract is the marriage itself; if the marriage does not take place the contract will not come into effect. A common form of marriage settlement is an agreement on the part of the wife to release her rights in her husband's property in exchange for a deed to property of adequate value.

Rights of a Surviving Spouse

Dower and Courtesy: At common law dower and curtesy were the names given to the interests of the surviving spouse in the lands owned by the deceased spouse. Dower was the right of the widow, and it consisted of the income from *one third* of her husband's real property during her life. In case of absolute divorce and other circumstances she could be deprived of this right.

Curtesy was the widower's right to a life estate in *all* of his deceased wife's lands. However, it was necessary for a living child to have been born of the marriage before the husband could obtain the right of curtesy. At common law although dower was not effective until the husband's death, curtesy was an interest which existed during the marriage.

In the United States there are at present many variations of common law dower and curtesy. A few of the states have retained them both as they were, but the majority of states have either abolished one or the other, or altered their extent. Curtesy has largely been abolished. "Dower," however, is now sometimes used in reference to the husband as well as the wife, and grants him a third or, in some states, a half, of the income from the deceased's real estate for his life. In a few states, such as FLORIDA, dower is more than an interest for life, being an absolute ownership in a portion of the deceased husband's lands. In addition to an interest in real estate, ownership of personal property is sometimes included in dower.

There are several means by which dower may be defeated. A property settlement between husband and wife may take the place of her dower right. They may contract with each other as to the rights of each in the property of the other, and if this contract is fair, it will be upheld by the courts. Where the wife abandons the husband without just cause, or is divorced from him because of her "misconduct," she forfeits her dower.

25

Dower may be barred by Will. Unless a Will clearly and expressly states that the widow (or widower) is to have both dower and the property indicated by the Will, it is understood that the provision in the Will takes the place of dower. In all but a few states, the surviving spouse, if dissatisfied with the terms of the Will, is permitted to make an election to take dower instead of the testamentary disposition. The election must be filed with the court within a certain period of time, usually six months after the Will has been offered for probate. Where there is no statutory provision for dower, the dissatisfied spouse may elect to take property determined by the laws covering the situation where the deceased leaves no Will.

These laws of "intestate succession" (which come into effect when the decedent has left no Will) vary in the different states. However, they all depend upon the closeness of the relationship of those surviving to the deceased person. Generally, a spouse or children take precedence over other relatives.

Homestead: Another statutory departure from the common law rules vesting all marital property in the husband is that known as the "homestead exemption." This idea also originated in the Republic of TEXAS, in 1839. The homestead is a piece of real estate whose value and size is limited by statute, which is specifically set aside as the family home. It is protected by law from attachment by most creditors.

The husband, as the head of the family, is usually given the right to select the homestead, but the wife may be so empowered where the husband has failed to do so. It may be selected from the separate real estate of either husband or wife or, in community property states, from the common property of the marriage. Any person who is the head of a family is entitled to a homestead in most states.

In addition to freedom from liability for most debts, the most important feature of the homestead laws is the protection of this property from destruction by one of the spouses. A husband and wife must join in any conveyance thereof, or openly agree to abandon it as a homestead. One

26

spouse may not bar the other, or the children of the marriage, from the use of the premises, except in those cases of divorce or separation where it has been given to one of the parties by order of a court. Upon the death of husband or wife, the survivor has a vested interest in the homestead. This may be a life estate in the whole property, which descends to the decedent's heirs upon the death of the surviving spouse, or it may be an interest in fee absolute. In any event, the survivor is protected from deprivation of the homestead by testamentary disposal; if an attempt has been made to will it away, the remaining spouse may elect to take against the Will. Where no homestead has been selected before death, in community property states the court will select a "probate homestead" out of the community property.

Family Allowances: The laws of a number of states have given further consideration to the support of a surviving spouse by minor allowances out of the deceased's estate to the surviving spouse and children. These allowances generally cannot be defeated by Will, and become charges upon the estate, whether thereby it is solvent or not. Sometimes they are subject to funeral and administration expenses. Some states provide for this support by the setting apart of personal property, in addition to recognizing the right of the family to certain articles such as household furniture and clothing.

Maintenance is usually provided for the family in this manner for a certain limited time, six months to a year in most cases.

Chapter III

RESTRAINTS UPON MARRIAGE

We have seen that the creation of a marriage is not always a simple act but is rather strictly governed by state laws. In addition to the requirements of proper age and physical and mental capacity, there have always been restraints upon marriage which, if violated, render the resulting attempt at a marriage status completely void, or render the resulting marriage voidable.

It will be necessary to here consider the difference between a void mariage and a marriage that is merely voidable. A void marriage is no marriage at all and requires no legal action to have it set aside, while a voidable marriage is one that is lacking in one or more of the essential elements necessary to create a valid marriage but remains in effect until it is annuled.

Marriages between persons who are related to each other in certain specific degrees are prohibited by all of the state statutes, although these vary greatly in the prohibited degrees of relationship. All of our states prohibit marriage between a person and his father or mother, daughter or son, grandmother or grandfather, granddaughter or grandson, aunt or uncle, niece or nephew and sister or brother. These prohibiting statutes are generally applied to relatives of the half blood as well as to those of the whole blood. The fact that the relationship is illegitimate does not affect the prohibition.

There has been prohibition of marriage between closely related persons since early Christianity and even some uncivilized peoples regard these unions as grossly indecent. The reason that such marriages have been legislated against are both spiritual and practical. From the practical point of view, a marriage between closely related persons may cause complications regarding the rights and disposition of the parties of their respective property. As we know, every state has its own laws of inheritance which are based on long years of precedent in addition to the present statutory laws. An untold number of entanglements might result from these marriages.

Another objection to intermarriage between relatives is that it has been found that the offspring from such marriages may inherit the worst traits of both parents. These traits, instead of being offset by others, might be accentuated in these offspring and if the marriages persisted we might have characteristics such as were found among the royal European families in the middle ages.

From a glance at Table 111 which illustrates the laws of all of the states we find that there are widely differing views as to which marriages should be prohibited. In some, such as the District of Columbia and Massachusetts, even those marriages between people who are related to each other only by marriage are prohibited. In others, as in Connecticut and Michigan, the laws are more lenient.

Whether marriages between closely related persons are void or voidable depends upon the interpretation of the statutes. In those states which list incest (marriage within a prohibited degree) as one of the grounds for annulment it would seem that the marriages are not considered void but voidable since there must be a legal action in order to set them aside. One need not necessarily be the injured and innocent party to ask the court for an annulment because this form of marriage is contrary to the public policy of must jurisdictions.

Even where the statute specifically states that marriages between related persons are void, such as that of North Carolina, there may be a mitigating provision. The present law of North Carolina states that all marriages between two persons of nearer kin than first cousins shall be void: provided, double first cousins may not marry, and provided further that no marriage followed by cohabitation and the birth of issue shall be declared void after the death of either of the parties for such cause (the cause here being interrelated marriage).

However, where the statute provides that a marriage within certain prohibited degrees shall be void and where the criminal statutes of that state provide penalties for disobeying this law, the marriage is not voidable until set aside but void in its inception. Does this mean that the state keeps a watchful eye on all marriages so that these seldom occur? Not necessarily, but if a marriage is prohibited by law and is entered into by the parties there may be unforsen consequences. Most pension plans and social security benefits for spouses of the insured person depend upon a valid marriage and a marriage may be looked into more closely if one party is an applicant for such benefits than under other circumstances. Another consequence might be a conflict with the laws of inheritance; a claimant to an estate may attempt to have a marriage declared void if he will benefit thereby, if it was one of the marriages prohibited by law.

Suppose that a marriage between related persons was entered into in a state where the particular relationship was not prohibited and then the parties moved into a state where their marriage would have been contrary to statute. Would this marriage still be a good marriage? This would depend upon the intention of the parties. If they were residents of the state in which they were married and intended to make that state their residence but later moved into the second state, the marriage would be upheld if the relationship was not considered repugnant to state policy. However, if the parties went out of the state in order to circumvent the laws of that state but returned to set up residence there, their act in marrying would be considered an evasion of the law and their marriage might not be recognized.

In one such case in Illinois, were the marriage of first cousins is prohibited, the parties, who were first cousins, went into another state to be married but never gave up residence in Illinois. Subsequently the husband was killed while in the course of his employment, he having been employed by a railroad company. A cause of action accrued to the representative of his estate and was brought against the company. The court permitted recovery only on behalf of the son of the parties but held that there was no widow beneficiary because of the fact that the marriage of first cousins is void in Illinois. The general rule that a marriage valid where solemnized is valid everywhere had no application here.

The Illinois Uniform Marriage Evasion Act states: if any person residing and intending to continue to reside in this state and who is disabled or prohibited from contracting marriage under the laws of this state shall go into another state or country and there contracts a marriage prohibited and declared void by the laws of this state such marriage shall be null and void for all purposes in this state with the same effect as though such prohibited marriage had been entered into in this state. A number of our states take the same view of marriages contracted with the intent of evading the laws, although at this time there is no uniform marriage evasion law which was adopted by all of the states.

Another restraint upon marriage is the prohibition against interracial marriage. A great many states have laws prohibiting marriage between white and black persons; these include Alabama, Arkansas, Delaware, Florida, Idaho, Indiana, Kentucky, Oklahoma, Tennessee, Texas, Virginia and West Virginia. Some of the statutes are worded to include other races, such as the Georgia statute which states that a marriage is prohibited between a white person and a person of any other race. Arizona and Wyoming prohibit marriage between a white person and a negro, Hindo, Malay or Mongolian while North Carolina and South Carolina prohibit marriage betwen a white person and a negro or Indian.

Some of the statutes specify the degree of color against which the prohibition extends. Florida and Indiana prohibit marriage between a white person and a person who has more than one eighth of negro blood. Kentucky prohibits marriage between a white person and a negro or mulatto, mulatto being defined as a person who is one quarter colored.

These laws have been upheld by state courts as not being contrary to the Fourteenth Amendment to the Constitution of the United States which gave all races political freedom. A large body of cases decided by the courts of some of the southern states held that the Fourteenth Amendment was enacted only for the purpose of granting political freedom and was not intended to prohibit social restraints.

Here too we have the problem of whether a marriage contracted in a state where there is no law against miscegenation would be valid in a state which has such laws. The majority of the southern states have treated these marriages as against public policy and have held them to be invalid even though the parties to such a marriage had been married in another state or country and had resided there as man and wife for many years.

Some of the statutes prohibiting miscegenation have the added provision that it is a crime for a person to go out of the state in order to evade the marriage laws of that state and then return to take up residence. In West Virginia, for example, this is considered a misdemeanor and the parties are subject to prosecution by the state. In Virginia this form of evasion of the marriage laws is a felony, a felony being a more serious crime than a misdemeanor.

There has been such a case in Virginia recently. A Black and a white person, residents of Virginia, went out of the state to be married but returned to set up residence there. The parties were convicted in the Circuit Court and an appeal was taken to the Supreme Court of Appeals of Virginia. The case is presently pending and has not yet been decided.

In 1964 the Civil Rights Act was passed by our Federal government. The purpose of this act was to enforce the constitutional right to vote, to confer on the district courts the right to provide injunctive relief against discrimination in public accommodations, to protect constitutional rights in public facilities and public education, to prevent discrimination in federally assisted programs, to establish a Commission on equal employment and for other purposes.

Under these new laws, if a case has been commenced in any court of the United States by a person seeking relief from the denial of equal protection of the law under the Fourteenth Amendment to the Constitution on account of race, color, religion or national origin, the Attorney General of the United States may intervene on behalf of the United States if he believes that the case is of general public importance.

Table III.

DEGREES OF RELATIONSHIP WITHIN WHICH MARRIAGES ARE PROHIBITED

Relationships within which a man (or woman within corresponding degrees) is prohibited from marriage:

	All States
	Grandmother
	Mother
	Daughter
	Granddaughter
	Aunt
	Niece
	Sister
	Half-sister
ALABAMA:	Step-mother
	Step-daughter
	Wife's granddaughter
	Daughter-in-law
ALASKA:	Grand-aunt
	First Cousin
	Grand-niece
	First Cousin once removed
	Second Cousin
ARIZONA:	First Cousin
ARKANSAS:	First Cousin
DELAWARE:	First Cousin

DISTRICT OF COLUMBIA:	Step-mother
	Step-daughter
	Step-grandmother
	Grandson's wife
	Mother-in-law
	Wife's grandmother
	Wife's granddaughter
	Daughter-in-law
GEORGIA:	Step-mother
	Step-daughter
	Mother-in-law
	Grandmother
	Daughter-in-law
IDAHO:	First Cousin
ILLINOIS:	First Cousin
INDIANA:	Grand-aunt
	First Cousin
	Grand-niece
	First Cousin once removed
IOWA:	First Cousin
	Step-mother
	Step-daughter
	Grandson's wife
	Mother-in-law
	Daughter-in-law
KANSAS:	First Cousin
KENTUCKY:	First Cousin
	Grand-aunt
	Grand-niece
	First Cousin once removed
LOUISIANA:	First Cousin
MAINE:	Step-mother
	Step-daughter
	Grandfather's wife
	Grandson's wife
	Mother-in-law
	Wife's grandmother
	Wife's granddaughter
	Daughter-in-law

MARYLAND:	Step-mother
	Step-daughter
	Grandfather's wife
	Grandson's wife
	Mother-in-law
	Wife's grandmother
	Wife's granddaughter
	Daughter-in-law

MASSACHUSETTS:	Step-mother
	Step-daughter
	Grandfather's wife
	Grandson's wife
	Mother-in-law
	Wife's grandmother
	Wife's granddaughter
	Daughter-in-law

| MICHIGAN: | First Cousin |

MINNESOTA:	Grand-aunt
	First Cousin
	Grand-niece
	First Cousin once removed

MISSISSIPPI:	First Cousin
	Step-mother
	Step-daughter

| MISSOURI: | First Cousin |

| MONTANA: | First Cousin |

| NEBRASKA: | First Cousin |

NEVADA:	First Cousin
	Grand-aunt
	Grand-niece
	First Cousin once removed

NEW HAMPSHIRE:	First Cousin
	Step-mother
	Step-daughter
	Grandson's wife
	Mother-in-law
	Daughter-in-law

NORTH CAROLINA:	First Cousin
	Double First Cousin
NORTH DAKOTA:	First Cousin
OHIO:	Grand-aunt
	First Cousin
	Grand-niece
	First Cousin once removed
OKLAHOMA:	First Cousin
	Step-mother
	Step-daughter
OREGON:	Grand-aunt
	Grand-niece
	First Cousin
PENNSYLVANIA:	First Cousin
	Step-mother
	Step-daughter
	Wife's granddaughter
	Daughter-in-law
RHODE ISLAND:	Step-mother
	Step-daugher
	Grandfather's wife
	Grandson's wife
	Mother-in-law
	Wife's grandmother
	Wife's granddaughter
	Daughter-in-law
SOUTH CAROLINA:	Step-mother
	Step-daughter
	Grandfather's wife
	Grandson's wife
	Mother-in-law
	Wife's grandmother
	Wife's granddaughter
	Daughter-in-law

SOUTH DAKOTA:	First Cousin
	First Cousin once removed
	Step-mother
	Step-daughter
TENNESSEE:	Grand-niece
	Step-mother
	Grandfather's Wife
	Wife's Grandmother
	Wife's Granddaughter
	Daughter-in-law
TEXAS:	Step-mother
	Step-daughter
	Wife's Granddaughter
	Daughter-in-law
UTAH:	Grand-aunt
	Grand-niece
	First Cousin
VERMONT:	Step-mother
	Step-daughter
	Grandfather's Wife
	Grandson's Wife
	Mother-in-law
	Wife's Grandmother
	Wife's Granddaughter
	Daughter-in-law
VIRGINIA:	Step-mother
	Daughter-in-law
	Step-daughter
	Wife's Niece
WASHINGTON:	First Cousin
	First Cousin once removed
	Grand-aunt
	Grand-niece
WEST VIRGINIA:	First Cousin
	Double First Cousin

WISCONSIN:	First Cousin (unless female is 55 years old)
	Double First Cousin
	First Cousin once removed
WYOMING:	First Cousin
PUERTO RICO:	Adopted Daughter
	First Cousin
VIRGIN ISLANDS:	Grandfather's wife
	Grandson's wife
	Wife's grandmother
	Wife's granddaughter
	Step-mother
	Step-daughter
	Mother-in-law
	Daughter-in-law

Chapter IV

RIGHTS OF ENGAGED PARTIES

Heart balm.

Those of us who were old enough to read the newspapers about two decades ago may remember the sensational "heart balm" cases. Many a girl became set up financially for life by either bringing suit against a wealthy playboy or by blackmailing him or his family by the threat of this law suit. Heart balm of course meant damages awarded to a person who brought action against another for the breach of a promise to marry. In those days most of the states had laws which enforced such breaches of promise. The damages awarded were sometimes extraordinarily high because there was no set measure to determine the amount of damages.

Eventually the legislative bodies of the states came into action and either repealed the law entirely or modified it so that excessive damages could not be collected. The Illinois statute of today, which was enacted in 1948 is a typical example of this modification. Stating that the law for the enforcement of these forms of action had been subject to abuses and blackmail the section of the Illinois law dealing with these cases reads: "Accordingly it is hereby declared as the public policy of the state that the best interests of the people will be served by limiting the damages recoverable in such actions, and by leaving the punishment of wrongdoers guilty of seduction to proceedings under the criminal laws of the state, rather than the imposition of punitive, exemplary, vindicative or aggravated damages." Damages in Illinois are now limited to the actual damages sustained. There is an additional provision in the Illinois law that the party bringing suit against another party for breach of promise to marry must give the second party written notice of such intention to sue three months from the date of the alleged breach of contract.

Before an action may be brought for breach of this type of a contract there must, naturally, be the existence of a contract to marry. As in all legal contracts, there is the necessity for an offer and an acceptance of the offer. A mere offer without a stated acceptance does not become a contract, and such an offer may be revoked at any time. An offer which is not taken seriously by the party to whom it is made, such as an offer made in jest, cannot form the basis for an acceptance of it and the consequent contract to marry. Therefore no cause of action exists in these circumstances.

All contracts are based on a consideration given by the parties to each other. For example, in the sale of a parcel of land, the consideration given by one party to the contract is the land and the consideration given by the other party is the purchase price of the land. In the contract to marry, the consideration given by both parties is the exchange of mutual promises to enter into the marriage status.

The consideration given for a contract of marriage cannot be an immoral one, such as the promise to marry made by one party to the other party if the second consents to enter into a sexual relationship before the marriage. However, if there has been a definite promise to marry, the fact that the parties have engaged in intercourse before the marriage was to have taken place does not invalidate the contract, and an action for a breach of this contract may be brought if the promise to marry is not carried out.

Promises to marry may be either oral or written, and the acceptance of the promise is evidenced by the conduct of the parties involved. Another similarity of this form of contract with business contracts is that the parties must have the capacity to contract. That is, there must be a meeting of the minds in order to form a contract and both of the

42

parties must have sufficient mental capacity to realize the nature of the marriage contract. They must also be without impediments which would prevent a marriage. Here again we see the effects of the statutory laws in restraint of marriage which would render a contract to marry invalid and one which could not form the basis of an action for breach provided that such circumstances as non-age, nearness of relationship or miscegenaction existed. One cannot make a promise to marry if the type of marriage contemplated would be one of those which is contrary to the public policy of the state wherein the marriage is to take place or where the parties reside.

Persons who are incapable of marriage because they already have a living spouse generally cannot be sued for breach of contract to marry. This holds even though the promised marriage was not to have taken place until after the death of the spouse. However, a married man may incur the risk of an action for breach of promise to marry if the woman in the case is totally ignorant of his status.

What about promises made by persons who are contemplating divorce? A promise to marry a person after the promisor has obtained a divorce is not ground for breach if such promise is not carried out after the divorce. Those promises made by divorce persons during the statutory period prohibiting remarriage may constitute a valid contract to marry. There are cases, however, which hold that these contracts are valid only if the proposed marriage was to have taken place after the period is over. We shall see in the book on divorce that a great many states prohibit marriage after a divorce for a certain length of time, this is sometimes applied only to the guilty party.

Promises to marry usually include a stated time and place for the occurence of the ceremony. If time and place are not mentioned, a reasonable time is presumed for the marriage to take place, and the home of the bride is considered to be the proper place. Where a marriage has been postponed for good reason, such as the health of one or both of the parties, there can be no ground for breach of the promise to marry.

There are certain defenses which the defendant may use to good advantage if he is being sued for breach of a promise to marry. The health of the parties is a vital part of the marriage relationship and if there cannot be a consumation of the marriage without damage to the health or life of one of the parties the promise to marry need not be carried out. Impotence is another defense to such an action. Insanity of either party will render the marriage contract void. The plaintiff's lack of chastity may also be a defense provided that the defendant did not know of this unchastity at the time the promise to marry was made or if she was unchaste with others. Intercourse with the defendant alone does not make the plaintiff unchaste for purpose of a defense to a breach of contract.

Suppose that a person has brought an action for breach of promise to marry and that the action has been decided in her favor by the court. Just what can such a person expect in the way of monetary damages? In states which have no modification of the enforcement of a breach of promise action the damages may come to a high figure if the social and financial circumstances of the defendant warrant it. The damages awarded may include recovery for mental anguish, damage to reputation and damage for loss of the status which the promised marriage would have brought. Where there has been fraud involved, that is, if the person who made the promise to marry had no intention of ever carrying out his promise, the court may award punitive damages. Aggravated damages may be obtained in some cases where there has been seduction under promise of a future marriage.

In mitigation of these damages, the defendant may plead that his motives were not malicious and that he had some good reason to break his promise. The aforementioned defenses to the action will be considered by the court.

Although the breach of promise action persists in some of our states, the following are among those who have abolished it: Alabama, California, Colorado, Florida, Indiana, Maine, Maryland, Michigan, New Hampshire, New

Jersey, New York, Pennsylvania, Nevada and Wyoming. Others, as Illinois, have modified it so that excessive damages cannot now be recovered.

As aforementioned, this action has been subject to such abuses that the trend of the legislative bodies of the various states has been modification of the law or abolishment of it entirely, leaving the punishment of such crimes as seduction to the criminal side of the law.

Engagement gifts.

Those gifts which were given solely in contemplation of the marriage between the parties may be recovered if the engagement to marry is broken. These gifts generally include the engagement ring and household goods. Other gifts may be considered personal gifts and therefore may not be recovered.

In Nw York State, which abolished actions for breach of promise to marry, a recent (1965) law provides that there may be an action at law for the recovery of a chattel, the return of money for securities or the value at the time the transfer was made, or the recission of a deed to real property when the sole purpose for such transfers was a contemplated marriage which has not occurred. The law further provides that the court may, if justice requires, award the defendant a lien on the chattel, securities or real property for monies expended in connection therewith or improvements made thereon. Instead of granting return of the chattel or securities or rescinding the deed the court is permited to award money damages if it sees fit to do so.

This of course means that one may sue for the return of property given to another in contemplation of marriage whenever the marriage did not occur. One cannot therefore, with impunity, obtain gifts from another under pretense of a contemplated marriage and then abscound with the gifts. The heyday of the adventuress is apparently over and the legislatures are doing their best to protect innocent people from the results of their own folly.

Chapter V

ANTE- NUPTIAL AGREEMENTS

There are situations in which the parties to a prospective marriage may wish to determine their respective property rights before the marriage. Sometimes this occurs where one or both of the parties had children by a previous marriage whom they intend to make beneficiaries under their Last Wills. In these cases a specific amount is agreed upon before the marriage which the wife or husband is to receive upon the death of the other, and by agreement before the marriage the one may give up his or her rights in the other's estate. The agreement may apply to one of the partners to the marriage or it may apply to both.

These agreements regarding property rights of a married couple are made prior to the date of the marriage ceremony and are called ante-nuptial agreements. These take the form of a legal contract which is bound by the laws relating to contracts in each of the states. In addition to a contract made between the parties themselves, a pre-nupial agreement may be made between the prospective spouses and a third person who agrees to settle property on one or both of the marriage partners either immediately upon the marriage or at some time after the marriage has taken place. An example of this might be the agreement of the father of one of the prospective spouses with them to transfer property to one or both of them upon their marriage.

We have seen in the previous chapter that there are certain necessary elements to a contract of marriage as there are in all contracts. The most important of these is the capacity of the parties to enter into a contract. They must be fully aware of all of the material facts and be without any legal impediments which would prevent them from entering into a valid contract of marriage. The agreement that is made between them must be a fair one to both parties. If the contract has not been fairly made it will not be recognized by the jurisdiction in which the parties reside.

While ante-nuptial agreements are made for the purpose of determining rights in each other's estate after the death of one, to settle an amount of property on one of the parties to the marriage or to effect mutual transfers of property, the purpose of the agreement cannot be one which is intended to defeat the law. According to the support laws of all of our states, it is the duty of the husband to support the wife. Therefore an agreement which is intended to relieve him of this obligation to support is not a legal one and will not be recognized by the courts. Likewise an agreement by a father to support his daughter after her marriage and which obviates the necessity of support by her prospective husband is illegal. Agreements made before marriage which are based on a contemplated future divorce or separation are not valid.

The consideration for the agreement can be the marriage itself or any valuable consideration. However, where the agreement has been entered into for the purpose of inducing the prospective wife to give up all rights in her prospective husband's estate, the adequacy of the amount must be a factor in determining the legality of the agreement. If, for example, the husband is worth over one million dollars and the wife has agreed to give up her rights in his estate for merely ten thousand dollars the agreement made between the two might be deemed to have been based on an inadequate consideration and might therefore be an unfair one to the wife. In the determination of the validity of these agreements, courts will consider the ages and experience of the parties, the amount of property which each possesses, their family connections, the needs of the wife and their conduct after the marriage, which might throw some light upon whether or not the agreement was a fair one. An agreement made by a prospective wife who did not have knowledge of her husband's affairs is not a valid one.

The agreement is generally required to be in writing and most states have provisions regarding the execution, acknowledgement and recording of these instruments. Some courts have held that the agreement must apply to a specific marriage while others have not, and have upheld its legality as to any marriage between the parties, who may have divorced and remarried each other.

The effect of divorce upon an ante-nuptial agreement might depend upon the fault of the parties, a wife who has deserted her husband or was guilty of misconduct might forfeit her rights. However, it is the general rule that divorce would not alter the effect of the agreement. From these facts it is apparent that an agreement should be drawn up so that the rights of the parties remain clear under any circumstances. It is customary that a phrase such as "the parties were living together as husband and wife at the time of (Mr. Brown's) death and — they were living together as such continually from the time of marriage to the date of (Mr. Brown's) death", which is found at the end of this chapter, be included.

What are some of the other factors which will render a prenuptial agreement invalid? If there has been fraud in making the agreement and misrepresentation by the husband as to his assets the agreement may be set aside. Any transfer of property by the husband to defeat the wife's rights which is made either before or after the marriage will also make the agreement invalid. Where the wife has been unduly influenced to sign the agreement or has been under duress at the time, the ensuing agreement is a fraudulent one and therefore not valid.

Those transfers which are made to defraud the husband's creditors cannot be valid. If the husband is insolvent or in debt at the time of making the ante-nuptial agreement with his future wife the law may well consider the proposed transfer of property to her to be a fraudulant one.

The courts will protect the wife who was to receive property under a pre-nuptial agreement that the husband failed to carry out after the marriage. If the husband had promised a transfer of real property to the wife and did not make the transfer within the specified time, the wife may ask a court of equity to impose a constructive trust upon the property. By this means the wife is assured of receiving her promised share.

In the case of a promise, made before marriage, to make a Will with certain specific provisions, which is not kept, the wife cannot seek legal action until after the death of the husband. When the ante-nuptial contract has provided that a sum of money be given to the wife in return for the waiver of all of her rights in the husband's estate, she does not forfeit her rights in his estate if the sum has not been given to her. These ante-nuptial contracts will be upheld by the courts in all cases where the contract was a valid one at the time it was made.

The parties to an ante-nuptial contract may wish to change the terms of the agreement after the marriage, or even to revoke the agreement entirely. This may be done with the consent of both parties provided that the modification or revocation does not affect the rights of a third party unless he or she also consented. When the third party is an infant for whose benefit the agreement has been made, it cannot be changed if the infant cannot consent to the change because of his infancy.

Transfers made by means of pre-nuptial contracts are taxable. The transfer of some of the husband's property to his wife is subject to the Federal tax applicable to gifts. This must be paid by the donor, but if the donor does not pay it, the donee is subject to the tax.

If the property has been transferred in consideration of a sum of money, the actual value of the property less the amount paid will be subject to the gift tax if the amount paid is less than the value of the property. Transfers made before marriage are subject to the whole of the Federal gift tax while those made after marriage are subject to only one half of the tax.

When the ante-nuptial agreement provides for the wife to receive money after the husband's death in lieu of her share in his estate, the money she receives is not deductible for estate tax purposes. When the contract provides that the husband will make a bequest to the wife by Will, the Federal estate tax applies, as does the state inheritance tax since the bequest is not deductible for tax purposes.

General Form; Wife To Receive Specified Sum Upon Husband's Death; Mutual Waivers of Rights in Property and Estate

THIS AGREEMENT made between [George Brown], residing at ...., City of ...., State of ...., herein called [Mr. Brown] and [Mary Smith], residing at ...., City of ...., State of ...., herein called [Miss Smith],

WITNESSETH:

The parties are about to marry. In anticipation thereof, they desire to fix and determine by ante-nuptial agreement the rights and claims that will accrue to each of them in the estate and property of the other by reason of the marriage, and to accept the provisions of this agreement in lieu of and in full discharge, settlement, and satisfaction of all such rights and claims.

Now, THEREFORE, in consideration of the premises and of the marriage, and in further consideration of the mutual promises and undertakings hereinafter set forth, the parties agree:

1. [Miss Smith] shall receive and accept from [Mr. Brown's] estate after his death, subject to the conditions set forth in clause 3 hereof, the sum of [$100,000] free of any and all inheritance and estate taxes, in place and stead of, and in full and final settlement and satisfaction of, any and

all rights and claims which she might otherwise have had in [Mr. Brown's] estate and property under any statute or statutes now or hereafter in force in this or any other jurisdiction, whether by way of her right of election to take against [Mr. Brown's] will, her share of the estate in intestacy, or otherwise.

2. Subject to the conditions specified in clause 3 below, the aforesaid sum of [$100,000] shall be paid, without interest, to [Miss Smith] by [Mr. Brown's] estate as follows:

(a) [$35,000] thereof within [thirty] days after the probate of [Mr. Brown's] will, but in no event later than [sixty] days after [Mr. Brown's] death;

(b) [$35,000] thereof within [six] months after [Mr. Brown's] death; and

(c) [$30,000] thereof within [twelve] months after [Mr. Brown's] death.

3. It is of the essence of this agreement that [Miss Smith] shall be entitled to receive, and shall receive, the aforesaid sum of [$100,000] if and only if (a) she survives [Mr. Brown] (b) the parties were living together as man and wife at the time of [Mr. Brown's] death, and (c) they were living together as such continuously from the time of marriage to the date of [Mr. Brown's] death. If [Miss Smith] does not survive [Mr. Brown], or if the parties were not living together as man and wife at the time of [Mr. Brown's] death, or if they did not live together as such continuously from the time of marriage until the date of [Mr. Brown's] death, [Miss Smith] shall not be entitled to receive any sum whatsoever from [Mr. Brown's] estate; and in such event, her waiver and release of any and all rights and claims she may have had in [Mr. Brown's] estate, as more particularly set forth in clause 4 hereof, shall be of full force and effect and shall be conclusive and binding on her.*

* This provision would in all likelihood be enforced if the parties were not living together at the time of the husband's death *because of the wife's fault.* But what if the husband deserted the wife, or she left him *with* cause? What if they lived apart briefly because of a quarrel but were reunited at the husband's death?

4. [Miss Smith] hereby waives and releases any and all rights and claims of every kind, nature and description that she may acquire as [Mr. Brown's] surviving spouse in his estate upon his death, including (but not by way of limitation) any and all rights in intestacy, and any and all rights of election to take against [Mr. Brown's] last will and testament under [Section 18 of the Decedent Estate Law of the State of New York], any law amendatory thereof or supplementary or similar thereto, and the same or similar law of any other jurisdiction. This provision is intended to and shall serve as a waiver and release of [Miss Smith's] right of election in accordance with the requirements of [Section 18 of the Decedent Estate Law of the State of New York].

5. [Miss Smith] acknowledges that she has certain property of her own. [Mr. Brown] hereby waives and releases any and all rights and claims of every kind, nature and description that he may acquire as [Miss Smith's] surviving spouse in her estate upon her death, including (but not by way of limitation) any and all rights in intestacy, and any and all rights of election to take against [Miss Smith's] last will and testament under [Section 18 of the Decedent Estate Law of the State of New York], any law amendatory thereof or supplementary or similar thereto, and the same or similar law of any other jurisdiction. This provision is intended to and shall serve as a waiver and release of [Mr. Brown's] right of election in accordance with the requirements of [Section 18 of the Decedent Estate Law of the State of New York].

6. Each party shall during his or her lifetime keep and retain sole ownership, control and enjoyment of all property, real and personal, now owned or herafter acquired by him or her, free and clear of any claim by the other.

7. The consideration for this agreement is the mutual promises herein contained and the marriage about to be solemnized. If the marriage does not take place, this agreement shall be in all respects and for all purposes null and void.

8. Each party shall, upon the other's request, take any and all steps and execute, acknowledge and deliver to the other party any and all further instruments necessary or expedient to effectuate the purpose and intent of this agreement.

9. [Miss Smith] hereby acknowledges that [Mr. Brown] has fully acquainted her with his means and resources; that he has informed her in detail that his net worth is in excess of [$500,000] and that he has a substantial income; that she has ascertained and weighed all the facts, conditions and circumstances likely to influence her judgment herein; that all matters embodied herein as well as all questions pertinent hereto have been fully and satisfactorily explained to her; that she has given due consideration to such matters and questions; that she clearly understands and consents to all the provisions hereof; that she has had the benefit of the advice of counsel of her own selection; and that she is entering into this agreement freely, voluntarily and with full knowledge.

10. This agreement contains the entire understanding of the parties. There are no representations, warranties, promises, covenants or undertakings, oral or otherwise, other than those expressly set forth herein.

11. This agreement shall enure to the benefit of and shall be binding upon the heirs, executors and administrators of the parties.

IN WITNESS WHEREOF, the parties hereto have hereunto set their hands and seals this .... day of ...., 19 ....

....(L.S.)
[George Brown]

Witnessed by: ....(L.S.)
                                             [Mary Smith]
....
[As to George Brown]

....
[As to Mary Smith]
[ACKNOWLEDGEMENTS]

Reprinted by permission from Lindey, Alexander, *Separation Agreements and Ante-Nuptial Contracts*, Matthew Bender & Co. Inc., N.Y.

Chapter VI

PROXY AND G.I. MARRIAGES

When two people are married by proxy, or by an agent, one or both parties may be absent at the time the marriage ceremony is performed. The absent party is represented by a person called a proxy who stands in for him and is authorized to act on his behalf.

During World War II a number of proxy marriages took place. Were these recognized in all of the states? From a review of the elements of a common law marriage it would seem that a marriage by proxy would be recognized in those states which permit common law marriage. This was true at that time. The marriage of a soldier or sailor from a state which recognized common law marriage who was married by proxy while on duty in the service was a valid marriage, no matter where it was performed.

It was a different matter for those persons in the service who came from states which had no common law marriage. There was a question of the validity of a proxy marriage for these people. The legislative bodies of some of the states realized that this situation might create hardship for these service men and women and therefore passed temporary legislation to validate proxy marriages. New Jersey, Kansas and Minnesota were among these states. There were marriages by radio and also by cable during the war years.

Some foreign countries, such as Mexico and France, recognize proxy marriages and these marriages are recognized in our states because a marriage which is valid in the state or country in which it was performed is valid everywhere provided it is not repugnant to the public policy of that state. A similar policy exists where a proxy marriage is entered into in a state which permits such a marriage.

At the present time the laws are somewhat different than they were during the war. A number of states which still recognize a common law marriage have no provision in their legislatures for a marriage by proxy. In fact, most of the state statutes have no such provision for a marriage by proxy or a marriage by written contract. Nevertheless, in some of the states which have no statute authorizing a proxy marriage these marriages are presumed valid. In Kansas these marriages are sometimes performed as they are in New Mexico. In Nebraska if a marriage has been performed by a religious sect which recognizes proxy marriage and if both parties to the marriage are members of that sect, the marriage is presumed valid. However, there have been no court decisions as yet on this matter. In the Virgin Islands the common law applies and therefore a proxy marriage is presumed to be valid there. Proxy marriages are also recognized in Puerto Rico. In South Carolina a marriage by written contract is allowed; when one party is out of the state the contract must be executed by the party within the state after execution by the absent party.

A 1948 New York State case upheld a marriage performed by proxy in Washington, D.C. In this instance the groom was in the service and the ceremony was attended by the bride and by the brother of the groom, who acted as his proxy. The ceremony was a duly licensed one and complied with all of the statutory regulations. The parties did not reside in D.C. but did reside in New York as husband and wife after the marriage. Upon desertion by the husband, the wife was allowed support from the husband by the family court.

In general, marriages by persons in the armed forces must conform to the laws of the states in which they reside. Whether or not a renewal of the proxy marriage will be permitted as it was in World War II because of the increasing number of our personnel overseas remains to be seen. Apparently at this time the services do not approve of proxy marriages.

Suppose that a valid marriage has taken place between a service man (or woman) and a resident of a foreign country who is not a citizen of the United States. Will the foreign person be allowed to enter this country and what is his status as regards citizenship? In World War II there was a special provision which allowed the foreign wives and children of U.S. service men to be admitted here as non-quota immigrants; application must have been made within three years after the termination of the War, that is, December 28, 1945.

These provisions applied to those who were married by proxy also. There has been several court decisions on the effect of proxy marriage on immigration which held the law of the place where the marriage was performed to be the governing law and therefore such proxy marriages would be valid here for all purposes.

After having been lawfully admitted for permanent residence, the husband or wives of citizens may file their petitions for naturalization after three years of residence in the United States.

A child born outside of the United States who had as parents one who was a citizen and one who was an alien becomes a citizen automatically if the alien parent became naturalized while the child was under the age of sixteen and such child was residing in the United States pursuant to a lawful admission for permanent residence at the time of naturalization or thereafter and begins to reside permanently in the United States while under the age of sixteen years.

From a perusal of the marriage laws of all of our states it is apparent that there is some variation, either large or small, from state to state. Marriage is not the mere exchange of the magic words "I do". Not only are the laws different, but one must keep in mind the fact that the law is a changing element, and must know the present law of the state wherein he resides in order to keep from an innocent evasion of the law. If one is contemplating a duly licensed marriage there are usually no great hazzards encountered since there are public officials to guide the prospective parties to a marriage in the regular procedure. It is the out of the ordinary marriages which might give difficulty, such as the common law marriage and the proxy marriage.

If the marriage continues and there is no separation or divorce it may be that the authenticity of the marriage is never questioned. However, when one of the parties dies or disappears the other party might find himself in the unenviable position of not knowing his status. Unless there has been a proper marriage the remaining spouse may find that he cannot inherit from the other no matter how many years the so called marriage has lasted. There has been many a deathbed marriage in order to provide for the widow so that she will not be without funds at a time when she may need them most.

The message which this text hopes to convey is that if there is any doubt in the minds of parties to a marriage as to whether or not they have been properly married or are entering into a valid marriage or one that may not be valid, these persons should not hesitate to seek legal advice. If one is not acquainted with a lawyer in the community there are always Bar Associations which are equipped to recommend lawyers who are versed in the law of their state.

Table IV.

STATES PERMITTING
MARRIAGES BY PROXY AND BY CONTRACT

Proxy
Marriages

KANSAS: Neither authorized or prohibited and sometimes performed.

NEBRASKA: Permitted if both parties are members of a religious sect recognizing proxy marriage and if performed in accordance with rules of sect.

NEW MEXICO: Opinion by Attorney General upholding validity of proxy marriages but not recommended.

NEW YORK: Not explicitly authorized but not contrary to public policy if valid in state where contracted.

TEXAS: Permitted where one party in Military Service.

PUERTO RICO: Permitted by means of mandate through special power of attorney.

Marriages
By Contract

MONTANA: Permitted if formerly acknowledged before a Clerk of Court and 2 witnesses and filed with premarital certificate attached.

NEW YORK: Expressly authorized.

SOUTH CAROLINA: Recognized.

Chapter VII

ANNULMENT

Historically the proceeding known as anullment of marriage was, in England, under the jurisdiction of the ecclesiastical courts as was the regulation of marriage. In the United States we have never had these eccliastical courts. However, those of our courts which are known as equity courts have a comparable jurisdiction.

What does the term equity mean and what, correspondingly, is a court of equity? Equity, by definition, means fair and just. Legally, equity is based on the philosophical concept of natural law which in reality is justice in its broadest sense. This concept of natural law has been applied to those legal principles which we know as equity. A court of equity, therefore, is one which is equipped to consider all phrases of the case before it and mete out justice accordingly.

The equity courts came into existence and grew up side by side with the law courts because it was found that law courts could not in some cases render adequate relief. The jurisdiction of an equity court is not marked by as narrow a boundary as is that of a law court. According to equity, there should be no right without a remedy. A court of equity has the power to make justice more complete in that it may grant relief where a court of law can not. Therefore, some of the actions concerning marriage came under equity jurisdiction because of the inadequacy of the law courts. At the present time in some of our states there is a supreme court or comparable body which has both legal and equity powers, while in others there is still a separate equity court. We often find mention in court decisions of equitable grounds for relief. In many situations concerning grounds for annulment the equitable grounds become apparent.

An annulment action may be brought either to declare the invalidity of a marriage which was void in its inception or to have a voidable marriage set aside. In the chapter on restrictions against marriage we have seen how the prohibition of marriage because of a too close blood relationship or racial difference made the resulting marriage void in some states. That is, there was no marriage at all. On the other hand, an example of a voidable marriage, seen in the discussion of licensed marriage, was non-age. If one of the parties to a marriage was under age at the time of the marriage he or she could bring an action to have the marriage annuled.

We may wonder why it is necessary to have a court action in order to declare a marriage void when in reality it is void. There are cases where the parties may be uncertain as to their respective rights in the marriage or they may wish to enter into a different, and valid, marriage. Therefore it becomes expedient to have a court decision to clarify the rights of all parties. There may also have been children of a void marriage whose rights and legitimacy must be determined.

Contrary to an action for divorce, for which the grounds are clearly stated by statute, the grounds for an annulment are much more complex. Here we might mention the fundamental difference between the two types of actions. An annulment action is based on the theory that there was some defect in the marriage at the time the ceremony was performed while a divorce action presupposes the existence of a valid marriage into which there later came some circumstance for which a divorce might be granted.

GROUNDS FOR ANNULMENT

FRAUD

One of the most frequently used grounds for an annulment is that of fraud, which is based on the theory that the party asking that the marriage be annuled consented to such marriage because of a misrepresentation or concealment of some vital fact by the other party to the marriage and was induced to consent to the marriage by reason thereof. The fraud that had been perpetrated must have been of such vital and material matters that affect the foundation of the marriage itself and must have been of such import that, had the consenting party known of it, he or she would have refused consent to the marriage. Since the state desires to protect marriage and is reluctant to treat it lightly, a marriage cannot be annuled for fraud in trivial matters.

Fraud may be either a deliberate misrepresentation or it may be a concealment of a material fact. In an action for annulment based on fraud, the respective capacities of the parties are considered by the court. The court will take cognizance of the age, education and worldly experience of the petitioning party and will look carefully into his or her background in order to determine whether or not the alleged fraud could have been an instrumental factor in obtaining consent. As may be anticipated, fraud covers a great many forms of deception.

1. Misrepresentation as to age, character and habits.

Generally misrepresentation as to these matters has not been considered by the courts as sufficiently vital to a marriage to render the resulting contract fraudulent. A court has recently denied an annulment where a husband failed to disclose to his prospective wife that he had been convicted for intoxication some years previous to the marriage, but another court granted an annulment where the husband had denied that he had a criminal record when he had in fact served time in the penitentiary for rape. The courts will also grant annulments in cases where there was concealment of narcotics addiction.

2. Misrepresentation as to financial condition and social position.

Fraud as to financial and social position is not usually a ground for annulment except in extreme cases. In one such case, the misrepresentations as to character were made by a person who was a professional swindler and in another case by a man who was a deserter from the army. In both of these cases the husbands had made the misrepresentations to wives who were very young and who were not in a position to be aware of the circumstances.

In a recent case in New York state the wife's allegation that the husband had fraudulently promised to establish a home and support for her, without which promise she would not have consented to the marriage, was considered good ground for an annulment.

3. Misrepresentation as to citizenship, nationality or race.

In those states which prohibit interracial marriage the courts would undoubtedly grant annulment where one of the parties denied that he was a colored person.

Courts are not all in accord on whether or not misrepresentations as to citizenship and nationality are sufficient grounds for annulment. Misrepresentation as to nationality has been denied as ground in some cases but in another case the misrepresentation of a person that he was a United States citizen when he was not has been so considered and the annulment was granted.

4. Misrepresentation as to identity.

Where there has been false impersonation of the intended spouse the courts will grant an annulment but where there has been assumption of a false name by the person whom the other consented to marry the grounds are not deemed sufficient.

5. Concealment of disease or misrepresentation of good health.

Concealment of those diseases such as syphilis or tuberculosis is a good ground for an annulment as these conditions would seriously affect the marriage relationship. No court would permit an innocent party to live as the spouse of a diseased person when he or she had been defrauded into a marriage by false statements as to the health of the other party. However, where cohabitation occurs after full knowledge of the disease the annulment will not be granted. Concealment of a minor disease as arthritis has been held to be no ground.

6. Concealment or misrepresentation as to insanity.

Since insanity existing at the time of marriage is itself a ground for annulment the misrepresentation of this fact will not alter the situation. Previous insanity or confinement to a mental institution before the marriage, if concealed, has recently been held to be a ground for annulment although earlier cases have denied relief in these cases.

7. Concealed intent not to perform marital duties or engage in normal relations.

The marriage relationship presupposes the existence of normal sexual relations and the bearing of children. Where one of the parties to a marriage has entered into it with the concealed intent to abstain from the normal relationship the other party is entitled to an annulment on the ground that a fraud was perpetrated upon him, provided of course that this intent was carried out and the marriage was never consummated.

In a New York case the wife refused to cohabit with the husband although there was no evidence of an expressed intention of this behavior before marriage, and the husband was granted an annulment. Naturally the subject of whether or not there will be intercourse during a marriage is rarely discussed before the marriage since it is considered an integral part of the marriage. Therefore the concealed intent to abstain must be construed from the evidence which is presented at the time of the annulment action. It has been held that the mere refusal to cohabit is not in itself a ground for an annulment.

A Michigan case presents a characteristic example of an undisclosed intent to avoid a normal marriage. The husband, who was the defendant in the annulment action, married a woman who had a considerable amount of property. Immediately after the ceremony he asked her for various sums of money, supposedly to pay debts. He himself contributed nothing to their joint expenses. He finally informed her that his sole intent in marrying her was for the purpose of obtaining money from her. After this disclosure the parties separated and did not cohabit from that time on.

The wife brought an annulment action against him. In its decision the court stated that a Michigan statute provided that where consent to a marriage was obtained by fraud or force and where there is no subsequent voluntary cohabilitation of the parties the marriage shall be deemed void. Voluntary cohabitation means cohabitation with knowledge of all of the essential facts. In this case the wife asked the husband to return to her and be a normal husband but he refused. The court granted the annulment to the wife.

8. Concealment of incapacity or misrepresentation of capacity to bear children.

If either of the parties to a marriage is incapable of bearing children and is aware of this fact, it must be disclosed to the other party before the marriage. The failure to make this disclosure is a fraudulent attempt to gain the consent of the other party and will permit the defrauded party to obtain an annulment of the marriage. However, if the party so incapacitated is not aware of his or her condition there can be no grounds for an annulment.

66

9. Concealment of premarital chastity or misrepresentation of chastity.

Chastity before marriage is not considered a vital part of the marriage relationship and therefore premarital unchastity is not a ground for an annulment. Concealment of previous fornication or adultery or even the birth of an illegitimate child do not necessarily constitute cause for an annulment action. However, a New York court did grant an annulment to a husband where the wife had stated before marriage that she was single when she was in fact the mother of an illegitimate child. But a California court did not consider the false statement of a woman to her husband before marriage that her child was the child of a former marriage when such child was actually the child of an illegitimate union to be sufficient reason for an annulment.

10. Concealment or misrepresentation as to pregnancy.

In those cases where the wife was pregnant by another, not the husband, at the time of the marriage and concealed that fact from him, and where he had not had intercourse with her himself before the marriage, the courts will grant an annulment to the husband. We find that statutes in a great many states provide for this contingency.

Where the husband had intercourse with the wife before the marriage there are two kinds of misrepresentation possible. The first is that the wife had become pregnant as a result of this intercourse when she actually was not pregnant and the second is that she was pregnant by the husband when she was in fact pregnant by another. In the first instance there will generally not be an annulment granted to the husband.

In the second instance the courts have been divided. Where the "clean hands" doctrine is applied the court will deem the husband who comes into court without "clean hands" (that is, without fault on his part) to be unworthy of consideration. In addition to the lack of clean hands some courts have held that a man in these circumstances should have been put upon his guard by the behavior of the woman and should have made further inquiry before he relied on her representations.

An extensive discussion of the above opinions has been given in a Connecticut case. In this case there had been intercourse between the parties before marriage and the husband was induced to marry the wife because of her pregnancy. After the birth of twins after the marriage, the husband discovered that they were the children of another man.

The Connecticut court, in its opinion as to whether or not the husband was entitled to a divorce (here the remedy was divorce although in a great many states the remedy would be an annulment for these reasons) on the grounds of fraudulent contract stated "His willingness to do all that he could to repair the wrong he believed that he had done her in being the cause of her pregnancy, and to accept the burden which his moral duty, under the circumstances as they were presented to him, called upon him to bear, certainly did not make his hands unclean in the matter of the contract from which he seeks relief, not for that matter as respects herself."[1]

This court did not believe that a punishment should be imposed upon a man for what was a laudable action. The husband, it said, acted as a reasonable man should have acted. To permit a marriage based on this type of fraud to endure would involve matters of paternity with its obligations as well as the right of succession to property. This case was decided in 1916. Fraud is still a ground for divorce in the state of Connecticut.

11. Concealment or misrepresentation as to previous marriage or divorce.

Some courts have held that misrepresentations as to previous marital status are grounds for annulment by the injured party while others have not. In one recent case a hus-

---

[1] Lyman v. Lyman, 90 Conn. 399, page 401, April 1916.

band was granted an annulment where the wife represented that she had been validly married when she had in reality been living with a man to whom she was not married; and in another case the husband was also granted an annulment where the wife had falsely stated that she had obtained a divorce against a former spouse when in fact he had obtained a divorce based on adultery against her.

12. Non performance of a premarital promise.

Some annulment actions have been brought because one of the parties failed to live up to a premarital promise to have a religious ceremony performed after a civil ceremony or to embrace a certain religious faith. Generally no annulment will be granted for these reasons. However, a New York court stated that the promise to embrace a certain faith after marriage might be a matter of extreme importance to a devout person and would warrant an annulment if the promise were not kept. The action must be brought within a reasonable time by the injured party. A New Jersey court also granted an annulment where the promise to have a ceremony in the Catholic church was not kept, both parties being of this faith.

One popular cause of action in an annulment proceeding has been that one of the parties to the marriage promised the other that he or she desired to have children and then after the marriage refused to have intercourse without the use of contraceptives. An annulment will be granted provided that the existence of the permarital promise and the subsequent failure to perform can be proven.

13. Marriage for ulterior purposes.

Marriage for the purposes of obtaining the property of another, of becoming a citizen of the United States, and for other purposes other than the usual ones of love and affection may be annuled.

An annulment was granted by a New York court where the marriage was entered into for the sole purpose of legitimizing a child born to the parties by reason of premarital relations although other courts have denied annulments where the marriage took place for this purpose.

14. Marriage in jest.

Generally a marriage that was never intended by either of the parties to be a real marriage may not be annuled if there was no fraud perpetrated. There have been some opinions to the contrary.

From the above examples of fraud in obtaining the consent of a party to a marriage it may be seen that these are many and varied. One cannot state with certainty, even in a given state, that a particular set of circumstances will be considered to be sufficient grounds for an annulment on this basis.

In those states where divorce grounds are few and severe, a great many people have sought annulments as a way out of an unhappy or unsatisfactory marriage. Courts have become less lenient in annulment cases because it has often happened that the fraud which was supposed to have been perpetrated by one of the parties is actually a fraud upon the court by both parties. It goes without saying that a party who believes that he has grounds for an annulment should consult an attorney who is versed in the field of domestic law.

In addition to fraud, there are several other grounds for which annulments may be granted. One of these is the non-age of one of the parties at the time of the marriage.

UNDER AGE OF CONSENT

The marriages of people who are below the statutory age of consent may be annuled. The annulment action in these cases may be brought by the infant or by his parent or guardian, depending upon the rules in the jurisdiction where the action is brought. Even though the person who was under age lied about his age at the time of the ceremony he may still bring an annulment action. In the event that the party who was under age at the time of the marriage voluntarily cohabits with the other party upon attaining proper age the marriage becomes a valid marriage without the necessity of any other procedure.

INCESTUOUS MARRIAGE

These forms of marriage, between persons who are related to each other by blood in degrees that are prohibited by state statute, may be annuled at the petition of either one of the parties. If this type of marriage is valid in the state where it was contracted it cannot be annuled in another state where it would be invalid because of state law if there was no intention at the time of the marriage to evade the law of the state where the parties resided.

UNDISSOLVED PRIOR MARRIAGE

Marriages between persons who have a living spouse from whom there has been no severance of marriage are void as bigamous marriages. In a great many jurisdictions this is a ground for annulment or divorce, even though at the time of the marriage the existence of the prior marriage was known.

Where a spouse has been absent for seven years and has not been heard from, the concealment of the marriage by the other spouse is not considered fraud. Some states, such as New York, permit a dissolution of marriage by the remaining spouse but there must be a reasonable presumption that the absent spouse is dead. This action is not an annulment action and not a divorce and it may not be brought earlier than five years from the date of disappearance.

Some jurisdictions have refused to grant an annulment for the reason of an existing prior marriage when it might be inequitable to do so. In one such case the annulment was denied when the petitioning party had continued to live with the other with knowledge of the previous marriage. In another case the prior spouse had died before the action was begun and the court decided that the second marriage should stand.

VIOLATION OF DIVORCE DECREE OR STATUTE BARRING REMARRIAGE

A marriage that was contracted in violation of a state law barring remarriage of a divorced person within a specified time period may be annuled at the suit of either party. This is also true of the marriage of the defendant in a divorce case who married the co-respondant, in those states which prohibit this type of a marriage. The "clean hands" theory does not apply in these cases.

In the event that the parties go out of the state to marry when the waiting period after the divorce has not elapsed the state of domicil will recognize the new marriage if it was valid in the state in which it was contracted. The same principle is applied when the defendant in a divorce case marries the co-respondant in violation of statute. The reason for this seeming inconsistency on the part of the courts is to prevent the undue entanglements that might occur, since it is a frequent occurrence that parties go out of their home state to marry when their marriage would not be valid in their state. The court does not consider these marriages as being repugnant to the public policy of the state as mixed marriages might be. The laws against remarriage have therefore no extra-territorial effect.

MENTAL INCAPACITY

A person must have the mental capacity to understand the meaning of the rights, duties and obligations of the marriage contract in order to be able to consent to a marriage. Mere weakness of mind or dull mentality is not deemed a reason for assuming that the party did not understand the nature of marriage.

To provide sufficient ground for annulment of a marriage because of insanity or idiocy it must be proven that this condition existed at the time when the marriage was entered into. It has been held by the courts that a marriage is valid when consent was given during a lucid period of a person who was insane. As has been mentioned in a earlier chapter, the mental capacity required for a consent to a valid marriage is not a very stringent one. A person may be well below average intelligence and still be deemed capable of consenting to marriage.

Although a marriage in which one of the parties was insane or incompetent at the time of its inception is actually a void marriage and an annulment is not necessary to put the parties back into their original status, it is considered an expedient measure. This declaration of a court as the outcome of an annulment action serves to clear any possible misunderstanding as to the status of the parties concerned. In some jurisdictions a marriage of this type is considered valid until a decree of nullity is handed down by the court of that jurisdiction.

Concealment of mental capacity may be ground for an annulment on the basis of fraud, provided that the party who conceals this fact is unaware of his condition. However, some of our courts have denied annulments for this reason.

There have been cases where one of the parties to a marriage was intoxicated at the time of the ceremony and was therefore not sufficiently competent at the time to realize the nature of his act in consenting to a marriage. Annulments in these cases will be granted only where the degree of intoxication was so great that it was impossible for the person involved to know that he had consented to a marriage and the consequences thereof.

73

PHYSICAL INCAPACITY, DEFECT OR INFIRMITY; DISEASE

Those physical defects which make the consummation of a marriage impossible provide grounds for annulment under most state statutes. These defects, however, must have existed at the time of the marriage and must be incurable. The lack of ability to have children is not in itself a ground for annulment unless there was fraud perpetrated on the other party because of a concealment of the condition. A marriage in which one of the parties has such physical defects is not a void marriage but is valid until it is annuled.

Impotence is another ground for annulment where the condition was present at the time of the marriage and where it is not curable. This factor does not make the marriage void but only voidable. It is necessary that the other party go into court and ask for an annulment upon the realization of the impotence of the other spouse. Until the decree of nullity the marriage will be valid for all purposes.

The term impotence means that there is complete lack of ability to enter into a normal marital relationship. The impotence may be physical or psychological and it must be in relation to the other party to the marriage. There is reason for this, since the impotence affects the particular marriage in question.

Concealment of a disease such as syphilis or epilepsy is, as we have seen, a ground for an annulment on the basis of fraud. Where the existence of the disease is known by the other party at the time of the marriage there can be no annulment. Although some states have laws prohibiting marriage in such cases, the resulting marriage is not considered void where there was knowledge of the disease.

DURESS

One of the vital factors necessary to being about a valid marriage is the free and voluntary consent of both parties to enter into the marriage contract. Even where both parties possess physical and mental capacity there may still be pressure put upon a party to a marriage in order to obtain his consent.

Duress means force, such force as to put the person concerned in fear of bodily harm. Here we have the well known "shot gun" marriage. Although the pressure may be brought to bear by a third person who is not a party to the marriage, most of our courts have held that this pressure must have been exercised with the knowledge of the other party to the marriage. Courts are divided, however, on whether the force imposed must have been such as to overcome the will of the person concerned or the will of a person who possess ordinary firmness of mind.

It is important that the force or threats of force continue until the time of the ceremony. Someone who has been threatened before the ceremony but who voluntarily goes to obtain a marriage license cannot allege that his consent was obtained by force.

Threats of arrests and imprisonment for seduction or for bastardy proceedings are generally not deemed sufficient to warrant a later action for annulment. Where a statute provides that a person who marries the one he seduced may escape prosecution the court will not grant a subsequent annulment of the marriage. However, where the seducer was young and inexperienced and who gave his consent to a marriage because of fraudulent threats, the court may grant relief by means of an annulment.

Chapter VII

ACTION FOR ANNULMENT

Having been apprised of the various reasons for the annulment of a marriage, we may now consider briefly the legal means by which one obtains an annulment. From a consideration of the previous chapter it should be clear that the annulment action is not always a simple matter. When so many of the grounds are based on the private intent and thoughts of the parties the subsequent court action may be quite difficult, especially in the matter of proof.

The fact that many jurisdictions differ in the grounds for annulment may also present problems. Here it is important to stress that a person who believes that he or she has grounds for an annulment should find a competent attorney in the jurisdiction in which he lives. Such an attorney will know the laws of his own state and, even more important, the decisions of the courts in that state regarding annulment actions.

Court

To which court does one apply who is seeking an annulment of his marriage? Since an annulment is primarily a suit in equity, courts of equity have jurisdiction over this form of legal action. In those states where there is no statute regulating annulment actions the courts of equity are presumed to have this power. When there is no court of equity as such, the supreme court or a comparable body is enabled to exercise equity powers.

Residence

Unlike a divorce action, residence in a state for a given length of time is not generally required in order for a person to bring an annulment action. The state in which the parties reside is the one in which the action may be brought. If both parties no longer reside there, the complaining party (who is called the plaintiff in court cases) may bring the action provided that the defendant in the action may be served with process personally. In this case the plaintiff would still be a resident of the state in which both parties resided. There is some dispute in the cases as to whether personal service on a defendant who is outside the state is sufficient to bring him under the jurisdiction of the court if he cannot be served while in the state.

If the parties were married outside of their state of domicil the courts of the state in which they were married usually have no authority to annul the marriage unless one of the parties still resides there. However, the state of New Hampshire is one exception to this general rule in that it will permit an annulment action in the state even though the parties left immediately after the marriage.

In actions dealing with annulment or divorce we find the word domicil used a great deal. This plays an important part in such legal actions. Domicil means the permanent dwelling place of the parties while residence implies a temporary place in which they may be living.

We have seen that the various states have different laws, not only for grounds for an action but also for court procedure. The ruling law in an annulment action is that which governs the courts in the state in which the action is brought. As has been mentioned, if a marriage is valid in the state in which it was contracted and the parties then go into another state and attempt to have it annuled because it is contrary to the laws of the second state, the court will not annul it unless it is a marriage which is repugnant to the public policy of the second state. We have previously seen how marriages contracted to evade the law are dealt with when the marriage is repugnant to the policy of the state in which the parties have their domicil.

Time for bringing the annulment action.

No specified time for bringing the action is given in most of our states although the action must be brought within a reasonable time after the cause of the annulment arises or becomes known to the party who is seeking it. In those cases where insanity is a ground for the annulment the cause of action comes into existence immediately after the marriage. In the case of non-age the annulment may be brought by the infant or on his behalf by a parent or guardian at any time before he reaches the age of consent. If the action is not brought, the marriage becomes valid upon the infant's continuation of the marriage relationship after he has reached the age of consent.

In the case of an annulment sought because a marriage is voidable the death of a party will terminate the action. Where the marriage was void in its inception, such as in the case of bigamy or incest, the marriage may be annuled after the death of a party by bringing an annulment action against the representative of his estate. This becomes a necessity in some situations becaue of inheritance or property right.

Parties to the action.

Generally speaking the aggrieved party may bring an annulment action on his behalf. Where one of the parties is an incompetent, the other party may bring the action against the incompetent who will have a guardian or committee appointed to protect his rights. In some cases the incompetent may bring the action by a relative who acts on his behalf. Where the law permits the incompetent to bring the action, either by someone on his behalf or by himself when he returns to sanity, the other spouse may not do so.

When a fraud has been practised upon a competent party to a marriage in the failure to reveal the incompetency of the other, the competent person may always bring the action for annulment. In all cases based on fraud or duress the injured party may bring suit.

When the marriage is a void one, either party may bring an action to have the marriage declared null. The "clean hands" doctrine does not apply in these cases because the state does not wish to perpetuate a marriage which is contrary to its public policy. As has been stated, there is also the necessity of declaring the rights of the parties.

Proof in an annulment action.

As in most legal actions, the burden of proof is on the party who is seeking the action. He or she must have the testimony of witnesses as well as their own in order to convince the court. There is a legal presumption that the marriage is a valid one and this presumption must be overcome before the annulment is granted. None of our courts will set aside a marriage lightly.

Results of an annulment action.
As to the property:

Although the effect of a judgment of nullity (which results upon the granting of the annulment) is to declare that no marriage ever existed, the courts will protect the property rights of both parties. Transactions which were entered into during the time of the marriage will be upheld whenever possible. Property which was acquired during the marriage will be equitably divided. There are cases in which a wife may be compensated for her services during the marriage. Sometimes alimony during suit as well as counsel fees may be allowed to a wife against whom an annulment action is brought.

As to the children:

All courts are reluctant to take any action the result of which will be to bastardize children. Therefore, even in those cases where a marriage has been declared void in its inception the children are usually declared by the court to be legitimate. Provision for their support and custody is always made by the court which granted the annulment.

Table V.

GROUNDS FOR ANNULMENT BY STATES

States in which there are no specific statutory grounds for annulment but in which a court of equity may grant either a declaration of nullity of a void marriage or a decree of judgment annulling a voidable marriage:

> ALABAMA
> ARIZONA
> CONNECTICUT
> *FLORIDA
> ILLINOIS
> MISSOURI
> OHIO
> RHODE ISLAND

States authorizing specific grounds for granting of annulment:

ARKANSAS:	Non-age, insanity at time of ceremony, fraud, force or duress, inability to consummate marriage.
CALIFORNIA	Marriage entered into as a jest or dare or while intoxicated. Non-age, insanity at time of ceremony, fraud, force or duress, previous marriage existing, inability to consummate marriage.
COLORADO:	Intoxication, non-age, fraud, force, duress.
DELAWARE:	Inability to give consent or consummate the marriage, non-age, prohibited marriage, fraud, coercion, venereal disease or habitual drunkeness or use of narcotic drugs.

*A divorce is the remedy where the marriage is either void or voidable.

81

DISTRICT OF COLUMBIA:	Non-age, insanity at time of ceremony, fraud, force or duress, inability to consummate marriage, marriage within prohibitive degrees of relationship, previous marriage existing.
GEORGIA:	Non-age, previous marriage existing, marriage within prohibitive degree of relationship. NOTE: No annulment will be granted when children are born or are to be born as a result of the marriage.
HAWAII:	Non-age, insanity at time of ceremony, fraud, force or duress, inability to consummate marriage, marriage within prohibitive degrees of relationship, previous marriage existing, existence of "Loathsome Disease."
IDAHO:	Non-age, insanity at time of ceremony, fraud, force or duress, inability to consummate marriage, previous marriage existing.
INDIANA:	Non-age, insanity at time of ceremony, fraud or duress.
IOWA:	Insanity at time of ceremony, inability to consummate marriage, marriage within prohibitive degrees of relationship, previous marriage existing. In the case of non-age, the marriage may be nullified within six months after the party attains the age of consent.
KANSAS:	Previous marriage existing, inability to consummate marriage at the time of the marriage, fraud, marriage within prohibitive degrees of relationship.
KENTUCKY:	Fraud, or duress, non-age, marriage prohibited by law, inability to consummate the marriage, inability to consent to the marriage because of mental incapacity or the influence of alcohol or drugs.
LOUISIANA:	Force or duress, marriage within prohibitive degrees of relationship, previous marriage existing, mistaken identity.

MARYLAND:	Incest, existing marriage.
MAINE:	Incest, insanity, existing marriage, non-age.
MASSACHUSETTS:	Prior marriage existing, non-age, marriage within prohibitive degrees of relationship.
MICHIGAN:	Non-age, insanity, fraud, force, duress, marriage within prohibitive degrees of relationship.
MINNESOTA:	Non-age, lack of understanding at time of marriage, fraud, duress, incest.
MISSISSIPPI:	Previous marriage existing, marriage between Caucasian and person of color, marriage within prohibitive degrees of relationship, incurable impotency, insanity or idiocy, failure to procure valid license (if there has been no subsequent cohabitation), fraud, force or duress, inability to consummate marriage at time of marriage provided no ratification of condition, wife pregnant by one other than husband (if no ratification of condition).
MONTANA:	Non-age, existing marriage, insanity, fraud, incest, duress, physical incapacity.
NEBRASKA:	Non-age, force or duress, fraud, insanity, imbecility or feeble-mindedness, inability to consummate marriage, existing marriage, venereal disease, marriage within prohibited degrees of relationship.
NEVADA:	Non-age, inability to consent, fraud, duress, or any ground sufficient to annul an ordinary civil contract such as mutual mistake, impossibility of performance, etc.
NEW HAMPSHIRE:	Non-age, and any other ground deemed applicable by court sitting in equity.

NEW JERSEY: Existing marriage, marriage within pro-
                          hibitive degrees of relationship, inability
                          to consummate marriage, (when not rati-
                          fied by other party) lack of understanding
                          at time of ceremony due to insanity, alco-
                          hol or drugs and not ratified, non-age,
                          fraud, duress.

NEW MEXICO: Non-age, marriage within prohibitive
                          degrees of relationship.

NEW YORK: Non-age, insanity at time of ceremony,
                          fraud, force, duress, physical incapacity
                          and inability to consummate marriage,
                          incurable insanity occuring after mar-
                          riage and continuing for five years.

NORTH CAROLINA: Impotency, interracial marriages, in-
                          cestuous marriages, insanity, non-age,
                          mistaken belief that female is pregnant.

NORTH DAKOTA: Non-age, former spouse surviving and
                          marriage in force, unsound mind, fraud,
                          force, physical incapability which incapa-
                          bility seems incurable, incestuous mar-
                          riage.

OHIO: Non-age, existing marriage, insanity,
                          fraud, duress, or marriage unconsum-
                          mated.

OKLAHOMA: Non-age or lack of understanding.

OREGON: Injured party may sue for fraud, force,
                          non-age, lack of understanding, or in-
                          cestuous marriage.

PENNSYLVANIA: Marriages which are void for any reason
                          may be annulled at suit of either party.

SOUTH CAROLINA: Lack of consent or other cause showing
                          no real contract of marriage entered (pro-
                          vided there is no cohabitation).

SOUTH DAKOTA: Non-age where parents did not consent
                          and the party did not consent or cohabit
                          after coming of age, living spouse, un-

84

sound mind (unless after reason there is cohabitation), fraud (unless cohabitation after knowledge of fraud), force unless cohabitation is free, physical incapability which seems to continue and seems to be incurable.

TENNESSEE:

Mental incapacity, non-age, duress by actual force or threat, marriage prohibited by law.

TEXAS:

Natural or incurable impotency at time of entering marriage or other impediment which renders marriage void.

UTAH:

Marriage is prohibited by law (e.g. incestuous), insanity, existing marriage, communicable venereal disease, marriage was not solemnized by an authorized person (may not be annulled if both parties believed the authority existed), non-age, any ground that existed at common law.

VERMONT:

Non-age if action started after plaintiff reaches age (cohabitation after age bars the action) idiocy or lunacy, physical incapacity if action started within two years, force or fraud.

VIRGINIA:

Living spouse, physical or mental causes deter entering into marriage state, lawful adjudication of insanity, or feeblemindedness, prohibitive degrees of relationship, and for any reason for which the marriage might be declared void.

WASHINGTON:

There is no specific statute dealing with annulment, but marriages may be declared invalid for non-age, prior undissolved marriage, incest, inability to consummate the marriage, fraud, duress.

WEST VIRGINIA:

Former spouse living and undivorced at marriage, consanguinity, insane, feebleminded, idiot, imbecile, epileptic or venereal disease at time of marriage, natural or incurable impotency, non-age, spouse without knowledge of other convicted of an infamous crime, wife pregnant by other than husband and husband doesn't know, notorious prostitute, husband licentious without knowledge of spouse.

WISCONSIN: Incurable impotency or incapacity of copulation at suit of either party, provided suing party was ignorant at time of marriage, consanguinity, previous spouse living, fraud, force, coercion at suit of innocent, lack of understanding unless after reason person affirms marriage, under 16 years unless validated by compliance, at suit of guardian or party if marriage occurred without consent, provided suit started before party reaches 18 and within one year of marriage, any other marriages void or prohibited.

WYOMING: Non-age if parties separate during non-age and do not cohabit thereafter, force or fraud and no voluntary cohabitation after force or knowledge of fraud, physical incapacity at time of marriage.

PUERTO RICO: No specific statute for annulment: governed by general laws of contract.

VIRGIN ISLANDS: If ceremony performed in the district and plaintiff is an inhabitant when action is commenced, or if performed elsewhere, when the plaintiff has been an inhabitant for 6 weeks prior to commencement of action, on equitable grounds, or of void or prohibited marriages (e.g. incest, existing marriage, non-age, fraud, duress, impotency).

APPENDIX A

A Philosophy and History of Marriage

Those whom God hath joined together let no man put asunder.

With these commonly used words in the marriage ceremony of the Christian church at the present time two people begin their life as a married couple. Other religions of course have their own particular ceremonies and customs concerned with the beginning of a married life. Marriage as we know it to-day in civilized countries is the union of one man and one woman for life, and marriage embraces a number of rights and obligations, a great many of which are centered about the bearing and raising of children.

Our present day marriage is of course a monogamous one. Was marriage always thus or were there variations in marriage in different countries and in different tribes? Historians tell us that the primitive form of marriage was also a monogamous one, the pairing of a man and a woman who lived to-gether for the purpose of caring of their children and of sharing the labors which were necessary for their maintainence. This monogamous pairing is also found among many of the animals below man. It exists among the anthropoid apes and in some of the birds. The reason given for a monogamous marriage among primitive peoples is the usually equal number of males and females, as well as an attachment between two couples which become lasting in nature.

We have heard of the type of marriage that is called polygyny, which means "many wives." Polygyny exists in every part of the world to-day, chiefly among barbaric tribes and uncivilized peoples. In order to have a number of wives, however, a man must have considerable wealth, and in those places where polygyny is practised it is the chief of the tribe only who has more than one wife. In some African tribes the number of wives increases a man's social position as well as his economic one, since the wives do most of the agricultural work. A great number of children is also a reason for having many wives. It has been said that this was the reason for polygyny among the ancient Hebrews. A recent example of polygyny in the United States was that practised by the Mormons, who gave this form of marriage religious sanction. This was abolished, however, by a final decision of the United States Supreme Court which upheld the constitutionality of an 1862 Congressional Act. Polygyny is usually based on a series of monogamous marriages, one man entering into a separate contract of marriage with each of the wives. In some African tribes each wife lives in her own separate hut and cares for her own children.

In those countries where polygyny was not sanctioned, it often existed in the form of concubinage. The morganatic marriages of members of the German Royal family were marriages between a member of royalty and a commoner. The children of such marriages were legitimate but neither they nor their mothers could inherit from the royal father.

Another, although rare, type of marriage is polyandry, which word comes from the Greek meaning "many husbands." At the present time this form of marriage probably exists only in Tibet and in India. In Tibet a woman lives with several brothers who share the same house with her. The children of these unions are considered to be the descendants of the eldest brother only. Among the Nayars of India the polygyny is a non-fraternal form. The woman enters into a ceremonial marriage with one man but then lives successively with a number of men. When pregnant, she usually designates one man as the father of that particular child. The children inherit from their mother's brother.

Other unusual forms of marriage are marriage by capture, which prevailed among war-like tribes, and marriage by purchase. Marriage by purchase still exists although it originated in early times among barbaric tribes. It was also associated with the institution of slavery.

Although the name of "marriage by purchase" has been given to those marriages wherein gifts are given by the husband to the father of the wife they are in reality not this type of marriage at all. The gifts are symbolic of the services and obligations of the marriage relationship. In a great many cases among African, Melanesia nd American Indian tribes, gifts from the husband have been first given him by members of his tribe and are offered to the tribe of the wife, thus becoming a source of union of two whole groups of people rather than of two individuals.

The Southeast Bantu tribes are chiefly an agricultural and cattle-raising people. Therefore cattle are an important sign of wealth. When a marriage is arranged it is concluded by the payment of cattle to the girl's father. These cattle cannot be used by him as he wills but must be used according to fixed custom; he must give some of them to relatives of his daughter and some he must keep to be given to his son's wife. If he has no son he may use them to acquire another wife of his own. If there is a subsequent divorce occurring between the married couple, the identical cattle must be returned to the donor.

In some American Indian, Samoan and Siberian tribes the family of the wife give reciprocal gifts to the husband or to his family. In some of these cases, the gifts from the wife's family may exceed those given by the husband. If this were to be considered a marriage by purchase, then the husband would be the one who was bought.

A result of the concept of marriage by capture and wife purchase was the custom of child marriage. This usually consisted in the union of a girl under the age of fifteen years with an older man, which type of union is still found among war-like tribes.

In India child marriage developed under the influence of the caste system. Sometimes the girl remains at home, having been married in infancy, until she reaches maturity but sometimes she actually begins her married life at the age of nine. Although the British government has attempted to do away with these child marriages, they still persist and it is said that over one half of the girls in India are married before they reach the age of fifteen years.

Even among those peoples which permit freedom of intercourse before marriage, such as in the majority of savage tribes, nuptial fidelity is generally expected of a married couple, and there may be penalties attached to any interruption of this fidelity. The adulterous wife is often punished more severely than the adulterous husband. However, certain relaxations of the marriage bond are permissible and customary among some groups of culture.

In Europe in the middle ages there was a custom known as "ius primae noctis" whereby the wife was given to a man not her husband at the beginning of the marriage. This custom still exists in a great many savage cultures, and is said to be based upon superstitions connected with sexual intercourse and the defloration of the wife.

There is also the custom, especially among Eskimo tribes, where the wife is lent to another man for short periods of time. This may occur when a man whose own wife is pregnant is about to set out on a long journey which would be difficult for her; another wife is loaned to him for the journey and his wife remains at home with the other husband. Sometimes wives of cousins are exchanged for a certain period of time.

In some Australian tribes, a wife may be given to another man for certain occasions. This exchange is governed by the elders of the tribe and is not a compulsory thing for the husband.

As in our own laws of paternity where the husband is presumed to be the father of any children born during a marriage, the children born among these tribes where wives are loaned to others from time to time are considered to be those of the husband. These savage tribes do not attach any great importance to the physiological paternity. Here we see that the prime function of any marraige is the bearing of and caring for the children of the tribe or society.

Concubinage, the relationship of a husband with a woman other than his wife who is on a much lower social scale than the wife exists in some communities but is not present among primitive peoples. So too is prostitution rare among primitive people but exists only in higher cultural levels of society. These two forms of extra marital pursuit affect only the husband of the marriage and not the wife and are therefore not comparable to wife lending as found among the Eskimos.

Among primitive societies there is no such thing as an illegitimate child or a woman and child or several children as a family unit. When there is a child produced as a result of prenuptial intercourse the father is obliged to marry the mother of the child and therefore provide a family of two parents for the child. In those tribes where a child out of wedlock is considered a disgrace, the practice of abortion as well as the use of contraceptives probably exists. In those tribes which regard the birth of a child as a sound basis for the subsequent marriage there is no disgrace attached to this occurrence. The primary purpose of the family unit, the raising of children, is thus carried out.

In most family units consisting of a father and mother and children there is a division of labor according to the functions and capabilities of each partner to the marriage. The wife usually has full care of the children and the maintenance of the household and cooking utensils while the father's duties consist of hunting, fishing, building shelters and protection of the family against enemies. The partners to these marriages in most primitive societies are on an equal basis, as they are ideally in most societies at the higher levels of culture.

The family unit, although complete in itself, is not independent of the group as a whole. Most of the men and women have duties with other men and women which assist in the functioning of the whole tribe or group of which the family is a vital unit. There is co-operation among all members in order to enable the tribe to exist. The men hunt collectively or divide some of the spoils, and they share their garden produce with other members of the tribe. The women may work in groups in the same manner.

In most marriages the wife leaves her relatives and comes to live in the husband's community. However, there are some cases in which the wife remains at her home and the husband comes to live there either on a permanent or on a temporary basis; he may stay and work in the wife's community or he may merely visit from time to time. In the latter case he is in reality not an indispensible part of the family but he is a legal necessity to the matrimonial bond, if not an economic one.

Marriage is therefore a combination of elments, sexual and economic, whose main function is all society, no matter how primitive, is to provide a suitable means of caring for as well as creating offspring.

Among the societies of people who were not of primitive culture were the ancient Hebrews. Through the Old Testament of the Bible we are able to gain a great deal of information regarding their laws and customs. The ancient Hebrew society is important to us because it has been of great influence upon our present day society, among Christians as well as among Jewish people. A number of our laws concerning marriage and the relationships between men and women may be directly traced to the Hebraic society.

The family unit among the Hebrews was an extended patriarchial one, with the father as ruling head of the family. The unit often included sons and daughters with their respective families, as well as slaves, concubines and sometimes strangers who stayed with the unit for a greater or lesser period of time. Although the male head of the family had absolute power, the wives of the Hebrew civilization were not in a subordinate role. The Hebrew culture regarded wives as companions to their husbands as well as helpmates with the family occupations. The children of the family were strictly governed and were taught absolute respect for their parents.

Since the ancient Hebrews believed that the only immortality attainable was through their descendants, it was of extreme importance for the wives to bear children. When a wife had no children, the husband acquired other wives to fulfill this function. Other wives might be acquired for other reasons as well, polygyny was a general rule.

While marriage was permitted only between members of a particular tribe, there were restrictions against marriages between blood relations and some relations by marriage. A man could not marry his mother or step-mother, his sister, half sister, whether the father's or mother's daughter, his paternal or maternal aunt or his daughter in law. Marriage between cousins was permitted. It was probably from the Hebrew law that our own laws prohibiting marriage between blood relations and relationships based on marriage developed.

Because it was of great importance to keep the family line of descent intact, the adultery of a wife was a severe crime and, if proven, might be the cause of her sentence to death. Adultery for a man consisted in relations with another man's wife; it was not adultery for a man to have sexual relations with an unmarried woman. Adultery for a woman, however, meant sexual relations with any man other than her husband. While the punishment for adultery was stringent, there was a great deal of proof required for a conviction of this crime.

Marriage among the Hebrews was accomplished by two ceremonies, that of betrothal and that of the wedding ceremony. A bride price was given as a part of the betrothal ceremony. A betrothed girl was considered in some respects as a married woman and if she had sexual relations with a man other than her betrothed both partners to the act ran the risk of being put to death. Where there were relationships between two unbetrothed people they were usually forced to marry. The Hebrew civilization provided an outlet for a man's extra marital pursuits by means of the female slaves and also by prostitution.

Divorce existed among the ancient Hebrews. It was at first a simple matter for a man to divorce his wife, but in the eleventh century this was changed and there were specific grounds on the basis of which either a husband or a wife could seek a divorce. Remarriage of divorced people was also permitted although a divorced wife who had remarried was not permitted, after a second divorce, to remarry her first husband. This supposedly outlawed any possibility of wife exchanging. Although the Hebrew religion apparently did not approve of divorce, it was very prevalent at one time.

The ancient Roman family is another family unit which might be of interest to us. In earlier times, that is, several hundred years before Christ, this too was a patriarchal

94

extended family; the father of the household having the power of life and death over his wife and children. It was the father who arranged for the marriage of his sons and daughters who were not allowed to hold any property of their own. The father might even sell his children into slavery. Upon the death of the father each of the adult males received a share of his estate, and could either remain in the household or set up a new family unit for himself. At this time the families were largely agricultural and physical labor for the members of the family was a necessity as well as an admired occupation.

Women in Rome in those years were not considered as persons from a legal point of view. Every woman was under the control of a husband, father or guardian. Although she could inherit property from her father or husband the inheritance came immediately under the control of the man under whose authority she was living. However, while not a legal person she was, oddly enough, very much of a social person. She attended banquets and other social affairs with her husband and was in reality the mistress of the house, having full control over the household tasks, the education of the younger children and the slaves if there were any.

Marriage in early Rome could take place only between couples in the same level of society, whether patrician or plebian; marriage with a slave was not a proper marriage. Later, however, marriage between patrician and plebian was permitted, as was marriage between men in the army and foreign women. A woman was old enough to marry at the age of twelve and a man at the age of sixteen.

As in the present time under our laws, a marriage had to be based upon the consent of both parties. Even though marriages were arranged by the parents, the marriage was not considered valid unless there was mutual consent by the partners to the marriage. Marriage was a private affair and was not under any regulation by the state other than the restrictions as to class of society and age. It was usual for couples to first become betrothed, at which time the groom presented the bride with a ring to be worn on her third finger left hand (as it is to-day). There was a marriage ceremony some time later. The ceremony, at which pieces of cake were eaten by both parties in a religious rite, was preceded by a torch bearing procession which escorted the bride from the home of her father to that of her husband. Her husband then carried her over the threshold.

Divorce in early Roman times, although censored by society, did exist but was not prevalent. The Romans at this time, unlike the Hebrews, were monogamous and of course adultery was one of the grounds for divorce. In those cases where the wife had no children, the husband might adopt a son to become his heir.

When the Romans became wealthy as a result of foreign wars with the accompanying conquest of people and their property the mores of the society underwent a drastic change. Since the men had been absent for long periods of time during the wars, the women had taken over the households and had become influential members of society. No longer under the power of their husbands and fathers, they acquired a great deal of freedom. The laws regulating their subjugation were amended and they were allowed to hold property in their own right.

Wealthy women did not find it necessary to marry in order to have position in society and could live as they choose. While formerly children had been objects of desire in a marriage, with the breakdown of religion and of the worship of ancestors they were no longer a necessity. Wealth and its pursuit became the main goal of everyone and it was in this period that the lavish banquets were held and the huge extravagant villas constructed. Marriage for wealth or for political advancement became the vogue. Divorce became popular and easy and adultery was no longer frowned upon but was openly practised. However, as with the Hebrews, in later times the people sensed a decay in their society and sought to bring it back to a sterner regulation.

Laws were enacted to curtail the extravagant spending and to encourage marriage and the bearing of children. The childless and the unmarried were penalized in various ways, by reduction in the amounts which they could inherit and by loss of political favor. Divorce was again in disfavor as was adultery. Nevertheless, some of these laws did little to alter the behavior of the Romans and they remained in a condition that was largely corrupt.

It would appear that when the cultural unit, the family, lived under severe outer physical conditions the laws which governed them were strict and were designed to keep the family unit together, most likely for reasons of its survival. When outside conditions became less taxing, the strict laws were disregarded and the people used their freedom from hardships to foster their individual desires. The family as a closely knit unit then declined and attempts by the law makers to bring it back to its original state were in the main unsuccessful.

The Greek family in the fourth century was a closely knit one, marriage being based on family ties rather than on affection. The Greek idea was to keep the family inheritance together and therefore marriages were permitted among fairly close relatives, a man might even marry his half sister provided that they had the same father and not the same mother.

The women of Athens were practically slaves; they had so little freedom. A young girl was brought up in the family home and was allowed on the street or in public only for religious festivities. She was taught household duties by her mother and by the female slaves in the household; the Greeks had a great number of slaves then. Her education was limited to learning such tasks as weaving and spinning and perhaps some music. A married woman did not accompany her husband to other than religious ceremonies and when there were guests in the house the wife would help serve the food and supervise the slaves but she did not mingle with the guests. The only time that husbands and wives were together in a mixed group was at family gatherings.

Marriages were arranged by parents of the couple to be married and, unlike the Roman marriage, no consent was necessary on the part of the girl. After the arrangement of the marriage there was a formal meeting between the young man and the father or guardian of the girl at which time an agreement of marriage was reached. This was considered an engagement and could not be broken without grave consequences. As a general rule the girl became engaged at the age of fifteen or less and the man at eighteen, marriages rarely took place before the girl had reached the age of fifteen.

The actual marriage ceremony, which was a religious occasion, took place first at the home of the bride, where there was a celebration and feasting, the men, however, being seated apart from the women. The bride at this time was probably veiled. Later in the evening the bride and the groom were driven in a wagon to the home of the groom amid a torch bearing procession. The groom's parents then welcomed the couple; nuts and dried figs were sprinkled on the bride, who was given a piece of wedding cake made from honey and sesame. The following day the parents of the bride came to call, carrying gifts and the dowry of the bride which was given to the family of the groom.

Athens at this time was a society managed by men only; marriage was entered into solely for the purpose of acquiring a descendant, preferably a son, to maintain the memory of the father and to carry on the worship of the family gods. There was little communication between husbands and wives although the wife did have full control over the management of the home and the food supplies. A wife kept the keys to the storeroom and this for her was a great honor. Love was not a necessary part of marriage. When the wife had no son, the husband might marry another wife for the purpose of bearing him a son. Often a man would keep a concubine, whom he had purchased, and he might legitimize the children of this union.

Prostitution existed, as did a group of slaves, called hetairai, that were seemingly better educated than the wives. These women charged fees and the most popular became very wealthy, some even married prominent men. Because of the fact that marriages were arranged for reasons of religion and family and because women had so little opportunity to become interesting companions, the friendship of a man for another man, usually a younger one, became customary. Most of the love epics of the period were directed at beautful young men.

Life in Sparta in the fourth century was somewhat different from that in Athens. Young girls were allowed to learn gymnastics along with the young men. The Spartans, famous for their physical endurance, laid great stress on physical activity and the development of a strong and beautiful body. Spartan babies were examined by the elders and, if found frail, were left to die. Athenian babies also might be left on the streets to die if the father did not wish to keep them. This could only be done, however, before they reached the age of ten days at which time they were given a name.

The Spartan boys were taken from their families at an early age and educated together in groups according to their ages. They thus learned such fundamentals as reading and writing although most of the education consisted in learning to become perfect in sports such as wrestling and javelin throwing. It is from the lives of these boys that we have adopted the term Spartan. They were permitted no physical comforts and they were forced to become hardy or perish. This period of training was given them before they entered into military service.

Athenian boys remained at home in their younger years and were taught only by their mothers and the slaves. When an Athenian boy became older it was the custom to send him to school in the company of a pedagogue who carried his books and remained in the class room with him to see that he attended to his lessons. School was taught at the home of the teacher who charged for his services.

As in Rome during a time of war, with the Peloponnesian wars and the absence of the men from Athens, the Athenian women naturally acquired more freedom and now went out of the home into the public, as did the Spartan women before this time. The women became so extravagant that an official was delegated to curtail their excessive spending.

Divorce was possible in Greece but it was necessary for the husband to return the wife's dowry to her family if he divorced her, which fact understandibly had a curtailing effect. It was a simple matter for a man to divorce his wife, but if the wife wanted a divorce, having no legal standing herself, she had to ask the assistance of a man who was a kind of public guardian for those incapable of managing their own affairs. Violence was one ground for which a wife might seek a divorce but adultery was not.

After this brief glance at ancient family life, we now come to life in colonial days in New England. Life was harsh for everyone at that time. There were no slaves to do the menial tasks and the family had to cope with all the difficulties of beginning a new civilization on undeveloped land. These conditions affected Puritan society. The family was in itself an economic unit; most of the population lived on farms where they grew their own food and made their own clothing. There was no subjugation of women, who had to take on all manner of physical labor to help the men keep the family alive. Existence for single people was practically impossible and therefore the family often included unmarried relatives who took over some of the household and outdoor tasks. Because of the necessity for extra hands, a large family was a desirable one and it was quite common for a woman to have as many as twenty children. Naturally bearing so many children under primitive conditions, as well as raising them, took its toll on the colonial woman, who often died at an early age.

The father was the head of the family and although he did not have the power of life and death over his family, he did have extensive control. All of a wife's possessions upon her marriage became the property of her husband and if she had inherited property he had control of this also as long as they remained married. Children were brought up to be respectful and obedient; the Mosaic law of the Hebrews was followed by the early colonial settlers.

The Puritans had come to this country for the chief purpose of freedom from the prevailing church, therefore marriage was considered a civil contract and was performed by a magistrate rather than by a minister of the church. Restrictions against marriage of relatives were similar to those found among the ancient Hebrews; these restrictions extended to those related by marriage also. Since a man could not marry his wife's sister, the wife was spared the feeling that an unmarried sister living with the family might become a rival or a successor.

While the parents may have had a part in the selection of marriage partners for their children and their consent was essential for the marriage, the consent of the children was also required and they therefore could not be forced

101

into a marriage against their wills. Young people whose parents opposed their marriage could appeal to the magistrate of their town, who was the official who performed the ceremony, and he might then give his sanction to the marriage if he found that the parental consent was withheld for no good reason.

Although the Puritans had a very strict attitude towards any transgressions of their sexual code, they were more liberal in the matter of divorce. Divorce was not common but there are cases on record of divorces, both absolute and the type of divorce known as a separation from bed and board. Divorces were granted for reasons of desertion as well as for adultery, although the adultery of the husband in itself, with no other complaint, could not be used as a ground for divorce. It is said that their attitude towards divorce stems from the fact that marriages were considered civil contracts and were not under the domination of the church.

When a husband or a wife had died, remarriage was usually undertaken within a very short time, sometimes a matter of weeks, probably because the family needed two partners in order to exist in those difficult times.

An unusual form of family living is found in the Israeli Kibbutz. The Kibbutz is a group of people who live and work as a community; they do not have any private possessions and the product of their labor is pooled for the benefit of the whole group. Each member has his own tasks and each receives his clothing from a common storehouse; meals are taken to-gether and are prepared by some of the members. The Kibbutz is a complete economic unit in itself. These groups originated when Israel was a new country and Jewish people came there to settle from other parts of the world. It was found that a group of people could exist where individual families could not, especially since most of the colonists were farmers.

Although each member of the group is considered a separate individual and the individual is given great status and is free to consort with whom he pleases, there is definite pairing in the group of a man with one woman and this becomes in many cases a lasting relationship. No ceremony is performed which could be likened to a marriage ceremony, the couple merely exchange two single rooms for one double one and move their beds into this room. No act other than reversing this situation is necessary for a parting of the couple. Nevertheless, most of the individuals in a Kibbutz after a certain age do pair off in couples and their relationships are as lasting as is marriage in the United States at the present time; the percentage of breaking off of such a relationship being slightly less than our own divorce rate.

Children born to these couples are reared apart from their parents, with other groups of children. They are cared for and taught in these groups, by other members of the Kibbutz. However, they do belong to their own parents and visit with them every day. Family attachments are strong, a child obviously derives a satisfaction from having parents who are exclusively his own and who remain the same. In his group he must share his teachers and nurses with the other children, and his teachers change as he graduates from one age group to the next.

The Kibbutz has grown from a few such groups to approximately two hundred and twenty-seven with a total population of over seventy-five thousand. It would appear that group living and caring for children can be an economic as well as a social success, since more young persons are attracted to this mode of life every year. It is not a completely socialistic society since there is a definite family life in the group which is built on the relationship of one man and one woman and their children.

Having studied various examples of marriage and the family from the ancient Hebrews to the colonial family in this country, we may compare the institution of marriage as it existed then with the way it is today. In the early days, when countries were new and underpopulated, it was necessary for their survival for family groups to produce large numbers of children and this was accomplished, either by a marriage of one man with one wife or with several wives. Strict laws were enforced to keep the family as intact as possible and to prohibit deviations from the normal family.

When a country reached a maximum population for the amount of land it covered and when migration to foreign lands was not feasible or desired, the population number was kept down both by the wishes of the famliies then living and by the existing laws. The abandonment of infants as it was allowed in Greece would be unheard of in ancient Hebrew civilization.

Divorce, it is apparent, has existed from ancient times on down to the present, even though it was often frowned upon it nevertheless persisted. As women became less dependent upon the men in their families the divorce laws were liberalized in their favor. After each war in a state, the women gained more freedom and economic status. Little by little women have acquired the right to own their own separate property which they may obtain by means of inheritance or by means of their own earning power.

This equalization of men and women has undoubtedly affected marriage and the family. Perhaps it has affected the divorce rate by increasing it. Whether or not this is a good or a bad thing for society has not yet been decided. It may be better for children to be brought up in happy homes where one parent is missing or where another has been substituted by a remarriage than it is for them to be brought up among dissatisfied parents.

From all of our readings, however, it appears that the family and marriage as an institution has existed for thousands of years and is still the best method of rearing children. Even in the Kibbutz which is a more or less socialistic society, a child knows and loves his own parents. Having established the importance of marriage, let us now peruse the marriage laws of today as they are found in each of our fifty states.

This is to Certify that

On the____day of the week, the____day of the month_____in the year 56_____,
A. M., corresponding to the____of_____19___, the holy Covenant of
Marriage was entered into, in_____between the Bridegroom_____
_____and his Bride_____

The said Bridegroom made the following declaration to his Bride: "Be thou my wife according to the law of Moses and of Israel. I faithfully promise that I will be a true husband unto thee. I will honor and cherish thee; I will work for thee, I will protect and support thee, and will provide all that is necessary for thy due sustenance, even as it becomes a Jewish husband to do. I also take upon myself all such further obligations for thy maintenance, as are prescribed by our religious statute."

And the said Bride has plighted her troth unto him, in affection and sincerity, and has thus taken upon herself the fulfilment of all the duties incumbent upon a Jewish wife.

This Covenant of Marriage was duly executed and witnessed this day according to the usage of Israel.

Witnesses: _____
_____

קול חתן וקול כלה   של ששון וקול שמחה

בְּשַׁבַּת ___ ב

לְחֹדֶשׁ ___ שְׁנַת חֲמֵשֶׁת אֲלָפִים וְשֵׁשׁ

מֵאוֹת ___ לִבְרִיאַת עוֹלָם לְמִנְיָן שֶׁאנוּ

מוֹנִין כָּאן ___ בִּמְדִינַת אמעריקא הצפונית אֵיךְ

הֶחָתָן ___ בַּר ___

אָמַר לָהּ לַהֲדָא ___ הַמְכוּנָה

בַּת ___ הַמְכוּנָה ___ הֱוֵי לִי לְאַנְתּוּ כְּדַת מֹשֶׁה

וְיִשְׂרָאֵל וַאֲנָא אֶפְלַח וְאוֹקִיר וְאֵיזוֹן וַאֲפַרְנֵס יָתִיכִי לִיכִי כְּהִלְכוֹת גּוּבְרִין יְהוּדָאִין דְּפַלְחִין

וּמוֹקִרִין וְזָנִין וּמְפַרְנְסִין לִנְשֵׁיהוֹן בְּקוּשְׁטָא וְיָהֲבְנָא לִיכִי מֹהַר

כְּסַף זוּזֵי ___ דְּחָזֵי לִיכִי ___ וּמְזוֹנַיְכִי וּכְסוּתַיְכִי

וְסִפּוּקַיְכִי וּמֵיעַל לְוָתַיְכִי כְּאֹרַח כָּל אַרְעָא וּצְבִיאַת מָרַת

___ דָּא וַהֲוַת לֵהּ לְאַנְתּוּ וְדֵין נְדוּנְיָא דְּהַנְעֲלַת לֵהּ מִבֵּי ___ בֵּין בְּכֶסֶף

בֵּין בְּדַהַב וּבֵין בְּתַכְשִׁיטִין בְּמָאנֵי דִלְבוּשָׁא בְּשִׁמּוּשֵׁי דִירָה וּבְשִׁמּוּשֵׁי דְעַרְסָא הַכֹּל קַבֵּל עָלָיו

חָתָן דְּנָן ___ זְקוּקִים כֶּסֶף צָרוּף וּצְבִי

חָתָן דְּנָן וְהוֹסִיף לָהּ מִן דִּילֵהּ עוֹד ___ זְקוּקִים כֶּסֶף צָרוּף אֲחֵרִים כְּנֶגְדָּן סַךְ הַכֹּל

זְקוּקִים כֶּסֶף צָרוּף וְכָךְ אָמַר ___ חָתָן דְּנָן אַחֲרָיוּת שְׁטָר כְּתֻבְּתָא

דָּא נְדוּנְיָא דֵּן וְתוֹסֶפְתָּא דָּא קַבֵּלִית עָלַי וְעַל יָרְתַי בַּתְרַאי לְהִתְפְּרַע מִכָּל שְׁפַר אֲרַג נִכְסִין

וְקִנְיָנִין דְּאִית לִי תְּחוֹת כָּל שְׁמַיָּא דִּקְנַאי וּדְעָתִיד אֲנָא לְמִקְנָא. נִכְסִין דְּאִית לְהוֹן אַחֲרָיוּת וְדִלֵית

לְהוֹן אַחֲרָיוּת כֻּלְּהוֹן יְהוֹן אַחֲרָאִין וְעַרְבָאִין לִפְרוֹעַ מִנְּהוֹן שְׁטָר כְּתֻבְּתָא דָּא נְדוּנְיָא דֵּן וְתוֹסֶפְתָּא

דָּא מִנַּאי וַאֲפִילוּ מִן גְּלִימָא דְעַל כַּתְפַּאי בְּחַיַּי וּבָתַר חַיַּי מִן יוֹמָא דְנָן וּלְעָלַם וְאַחֲרָיוּת שְׁטָר

כְּתֻבְּתָא דָּא נְדוּנְיָא דֵּן וְתוֹסֶפְתָּא דָּא קַבֵּל עָלָיו ___ חָתָן דְּנָן כְּחֹמֶר

כָּל שְׁטָרֵי כְתֻבּוֹת וְתוֹסְפָתוֹת דְּנָהֲגִין בִּבְנוֹת יִשְׂרָאֵל הָעֲשׂוּיִין כְּתִקּוּן חֲכָמֵינוּ זִכְרָם לִבְרָכָה דְּלָא

כְּאַסְמַכְתָּא וּדְלָא כְּטוֹפְסֵי דִשְׁטָרֵי וְקָנִינָא מִן ___ בַּר

חָתָן דְּנָן לְמָרַת ___ בַּת

דָּא עַל כָּל מַה דִּכְתִיב וּמְפֹרָשׁ לְעֵיל בְּמָנָא דְּכָשֵׁר לְמִקְנָא בֵּהּ

וְהַכֹּל שָׁרִיר וְקַיָּם.

נְאוּם ___ עֵד.   וּנְאוּם ___ עֵד.

APPENDIX C

The Form of Solemnization of Matrimony from the Protestant Epsicopal Church Prayer Book

Dearly beloved, we are gathered together here in the sight of God, and in the face of this company, to join together this Man and this Woman in holy matrimony; which is an honorable estate, instituted by God, signifying unto us the mystical union that is betwixt Christ and his Church: which holy estate Christ adorned and beautified with his presence and first miracle that he wrought in Cana of Galilee, and is commended of Saint Paul to be honorable among all men: and therefore is not by any to be entered into unadvisedly or lightly; but reverently, discreetly, advisedly, soberly, and in the fear of God. Into this holy estate, these two persons present come now to be joined. If any man can show just cause, why they may not lawfully be joined together, let him now speak, or else hereafter for ever hold his peace.

(And speaking to the persons who are to be married, the minister shall say)

I require and charge you both, as ye will answer at the dreadful day of judgment when the secrets of all hearts shall be disclosed, that if either of you know any impediment, why ye may not be lawfully joined together in Matrimony, ye do now confess it. For be ye well assured, that if any persons are joined together otherwise than as God's Word doth allow, their marriage is not lawful.

Wilt thou have this Woman to be thy wedded wife, to live together after God's ordinance in the holy estate of Matrimony? Wilt thou love her, comfort her, honour, and keep her in sickness and in health; and, forsaking all others, keep thee only unto her, so long as ye both shall live?

I will.

Wilt thou have this Man to thy wedded husband, to live together after God's ordinance in the holy estate of Matrimony? Wilt thou love him, comfort him, honour, and keep him in sickness and in health; and, forsaking all others, keep thee only unto him, so long as ye both shall live?

I will.

Who giveth this Woman to be married to this Man?

(Then shall they gvie their troth to each other in this manner. The Minister, receiving the Woman at her father's or friend's hands, shall cause the Man with his right hand to take the Woman by her right hand, and to say after him as followeth.)

I, (name), take thee (name) to my wedded Wife, to have and to hold from this day forward, for better for worse, for richer for poorer, in sickness and in health, to love and to cherish, till death us to part, according to God's holy ordinance; and I plight thee my troth.

(The woman with her right hand taking the man by his right hand)

I (name), take thee (name) to my wedded Husband, to have and to hold from this day forward, for better for worse, for richer for poorer, in sickness and in health, to love and to cherish, till death us do part, according to God's holy ordinance; and thereto I give thee my troth.

(Then shall they again loose their hands; and the Man shall give unto the Woman a Ring on this wise; the Minister taking the Ring shall deliver it to the Man, to put it upon the fourth finger of the Woman's left hand. And the Man holding the Ring there, and taught by the Minister, shall say,)

With this Ring I thee wed; in the name of the Father, and of the Son, and of the Holy Ghost. Amen.

(Before delivering the Ring to the Man, the Minister may say)

Bless, O Lord, this Ring, that he who gives it and she who wears it may abide in thy peace, and continue in thy favor, unto their life's end; through Jesus Christ our Lord. Amen. Let us pray.

(The Minister and the people)

Our Father, who art in heaven, Hallowed be thy Name. Thy kingdom come. Thy will be done, On earth as it is in heaven. Give us this day our daily bread. And forgive us our trespasses, As we forgive those who trespass against us. And lead us not into temptation, But deliver us from evil. For thine is the kingdom, and the power, and the glory, for evr and ever. Amen.

(The Minister adds)

O Eternal God, Creator and Preserver of all mankind, Giver of all spiritual grace, the Author of everlasting life; Send thy blessing upon these thy servants, this man and this woman, whom we bless in thy Name; that they, living faithfully together, may surely perform and keep the vow and covenant betwixt them made, (whereof this Ring given and received is a token and pledge,) and may ever remain in perfect love and peace together, and live according to thy laws; through Jesus Christ our Lord. Amen.

O Almighty God, Creator of mankind, who only art the well-spring of life; Bestow upon these thy servants, if it be thy will, the gift and heritage of children; and grant that they may see their children brought up in faith and fear, to the honour and glory of ty Name; through Jesus Christ our Lord. Amen.

Those whom God hath joined together let no man put asunder.

Forasmuch as (name) and (name) have consented together in holy wedlock, and have witnessed the same before God and this company, and thereto have given and pledged thier troth, each to the other, and have declared the same by giving and receiving a ring, and by joining hands; I pronounce that they are Man and Wife, In the Name of the Father, and of the Son, and of the Holy Ghost. Amen.

God the Father, God the Son, God the Holy Ghost, bless, preserve, and keep you; the Lord mercifully with his favour look upon you, and fill you with all spiritual benediction and grace; that ye may so live together in this life, that in the world to come ye may have life everlasting. Amen.

(Note: The laws respecting matrimony being different in the several states, every Minister is left to the direction of these laws, in everything that regards the civil contract between the parties.)

APPENDIX D

The Marriage Ceremony of the Roman Catholic Church
Rite For the Sacrament of Matrimony
Versicle: Our help is in the name of the Lord.
Response: Who made heaven and earth.
V.: O Lord, hear my prayer.
R.: And let my cry come unto Thee.
V.: The Lord be with you.
R.: And with your spirit.
Let us pray. O Lord, we implore Thee, let Thy inspiration precede our actions and Thy help further them, so that all our prayers and all our deeds may ever take their beginning from Thee and, so begun, may through Thee reach completion. Through Christ Our Lord.
R.: Amen.

Instruction Before Marriage

Dear friends in Christ: As you know, you are about to enter into a union which is most sacred and most serious, a union which was established by God Himself. By it, He gave to man a share in the greatest work of creation, the work of the continuation of the human race. And in this way He sanctified human love and enabled man and woman to help each other live as children of God, by sharing a common life under His fatherly care.

Because God Himself is thus its author, marriage is of its very nature a holy institution, requiring of those who enter into it a complete and unreserved giving of self. But Christ our Lord added to the holiness of marriage an even deeper meaning and a higher beauty. He referred to the love of marriage to describe His own love for His Church, that is, for the people of God whom He redeemed by His own blood. And so He gave to Christians a new vision of what married life ought to be, a life of self-sacrificing love like His own. It is for this reason that His Apostle, St. Paul, clearly states that marriage is now and for all time to be considered a great mystery, intimately bound up with the supernatural union of Christ and the Church, which union is also to be its pattern.

This union then is most serious, because it will bind you together for life in a relationship so close and so intimate, that it will profoundly influence your whole future. That future, with its hopes and disappointments, its successes and its failures, its pleasures and its pains, its joys and its sorrows, is hidden from your eyes. You know that these elements are mingled in every life, and are to be expected in your own. And so, not knowing what is before you, you take each other for better or for worse, for richer or for poorer, in sickness and in health, until death.

Truly, then, these words are most serious. It is a beautiful tribute to your undoubted faith in each other, that, recognizing their full import, you are nevertheless so willing and ready to pronounce them. And because these words involve such solemn obligations, it is most fitting that you rest the security of your wedded life upon the great principle of self-sacrifice. And so you begin your married life by the voluntary and complete surrender of your individual lives in the interest of that deeper and wider life which you are to have in common. Henceforth you belong entirely to each other; you will be one in mind, one in heart, and one in affections. And whatever sacrifices you may hereafter be required to make to preserve this common life, always make them generously. Sacrifice is usually difficult and irksome. Only love can make it easy; and perfect love can make it a joy. We are willing to give in proportion as we love. And when love is perfect, the sacrifice is complete. God so loved the world that He gave His Only begotten Son; and the Son so loved us that He gave Himself for our salvation. "Greater love than this no man hath, that a man lay down his life for his friends."

No greater blessing can come to your married life than pure conjugal love, loyal and true to the end. May, then, this love with which you join your hands and hearts today, never fail, but grow deeper and stronger as the years go on. And if true love and the unselfish spirit of perfect sacrifice guide your every action, you can expect the greatest measure of earthly happiness that may be allotted to man in this vale of tears. The rest is in the hands of God. Nor will God be wanting to your needs: He will pledge you the life-long support of His graces in the Holy Sacrament which you are now going to receive.

The Marriage Ceremony
The Priest asks the Bridegroom:
(*Stand*)

N., will you take N., here present, for your lawful wife according to the rite of our holy Mother, the Church?

Response: I will.

Then the Priest asks the bride:

N., will you take N., here present, for your lawful husband according to the rite of our holy Mother, the Church?

Response: I will.

The consent of one is not sufficient; it must be expressed in some sensible sign by both. After obtaining their mutual consent, the Priest bids the man and woman join their right hands.

The man says after the Priest:

I, N.N., take you, N.N., for my lawful wife, to have and to hold, from this day forward, for better, for worse, for richer, for poorer, in sickness and in health, until death do us part.

Then the woman says after the Priest:

I, N.N., take you, N.N., for my lawful husband, to have and to hold, from this day forward, for better, for worse, for richer, or poorer, in sickness and in health, until death do us part.

The Bridegroom and Bride may kneel, and the Priest says:

I join you in matrimony, in the name of the Father, and of the Son, and of the Holy Spirit. Amen.

I call upon all of you here present to be witnesses of this holy union which I have now blessed. "What God has joined together, let no man put asunder."

He then sprinkles them with holy water. This done, the Priest blesses the ring(s), saying:

Versicle: Our help is in the name of the Lord.

Response: Who made heaven and earth.

V.: O Lord, hear my prayer.

R.: And let my cry come unto Thee.

V.: The Lord be with you.

R.: And with your spirit.

Let us pray. Bless, O Lord, these rings, which we are blessing in Thy name, so that they who wear them, keeping faith with each other in unbroken loyalty, may ever remain at peace with Thee, obedient to Thy will, and may live together always in mutual love. Through Christ our Lord.

R.: Amen.

The Priest having sprinkled the ring(s) says:

Now that you have sealed a truly Christian marriage, give this wedding ring / these wedding rings to your bride / to each other, saying after me:

The Groom having received the ring from the hand of the Priest puts it on the third finger of the left hand of the Bride and repeats after te Priest:

In the name of the Father, and of the Son, and of the Holy Spirit. Take and wear this ring as a pledge of my fidelity.

The Bride having received the ring from the hand of the Priest puts it on the third finger of the left hand of the Groom and repeats after the Priest:

In the name of the Father, and of the Son, and of the Holy Spirit. Take and wear this ring as a pledge of my fidelity.

Blessing

Psalm 127

Happy are you who fear the Lord, who walk in his ways!

For you shall eat the fruit of your handiwork; happy shall you be, and favored.

Your wife shall be like a fruitul vine in the recesses of your home;

Your children like olive plants around your table.

Behold, thus is the man blessed who fears the Lord.

The Lord bless you from Sion: May you see the prosperity of Jerusalem all the days of your life;

May you see your children's children. Peace be upon Israel!

Glory be to the Father, and to the Son, and to the Holy Spirit.

As it was in the beginning, is now, and ever shall be, world without end. Amen.

V.: Lord, have mercy.

R.: Christ, have mercy.

Lord, have mercy.

Our Father (*silently*).

V.: And lead us not into temptation.

R.: But deliver us from evil.

V.: Grant salvation to Thy servants.

R.: For their hope, O my God, is in Thee.

V.: Send them aid, O Lord, from Thy holy place.

R.: And watch over them from Sion.

V.: O Lord, hear my prayer.

R.: And let my cry come unto Thee.

V.: The Lord be with you.

R.: And with your spirit.

Let us pray. Almighty and everlasting God, Who by Thy power didst create Adam and Eve, our first parents, and join them in a holy union, sanctify the hearts and the bodies of these Thy servants, and bless them; and make them one in the union and love of true affection. Through Christ our Lord.

R.: Amen.

The Priest with hands upraised and extended over the Bride and Bridegroom says:

May almighty God bless you by the Word of His mouth, and unite your hearts in the enduring bond of pure love.

R.: Amen.

May you be blessed in your children, and may the love that you lavish on them be returned a hundredfold.

R.: Amen.

May the peace of Christ dwell always in your hearts and in your home; may you have true friends to stand by you, both in joy and in sorrow. May you be ready with help and consolation for all those who come to you in need; and may the blessings promised to the compassionate descend in abundance on your house.

R.: Amen.

May you be blessed in your work and enjoy its fruits. May cares never cause you distress, nor the desire for earthly possessions lead you astray; but may your hearts' concern be always for the treasures laid up for you in the life of heaven.

R.: Amen.

May the Lord grant you fullness of years, so that you may reap the harvest of a good life, and, after you have served Him with loyalty in His kingdom on earth, may He take you up into His eternal dominions in heaven.

Through our Lord Jesus Christ His Son, Who lives and reigns with Him in the unity of the Holy Spirit, God, world without end.

R.: Amen.

The Mass follows with the Nuptial Blessing.

Muptial Blessing; L. The blessing read by the priest after the Pater Noster of the Mass (Pro Sponsis), called nuptial, which may not be given apart from the Mass except with dispensation. The blessing is directed more to the woman than to the man. It is not given if the woman has received it at a previous marriage, nor during special times or seasons of the Church calendar.

GLOSSARY OF TERMS

Annulment of Marriage. An action or proceeding for the annulment of a marriage is maintained on the theory that for some cause existing at the time of marriage no valid or legal marriage ever existed, even though the marriage be only voidable at the instance of the injured party. It is therefore distinguishable from an action for divorce, which is based on the theory of a valid marriage, for some cause arising after the marriage.

Common Law. That body of law and juristic theory which was originated, developed, and formulated and is administered in English, and has obtained among most of the states and peoples of Anglo-Saxon stock.

Consideration. In contracts the cause, motive, price, or impelling influence which induces a contracting party to enter into a contract.

Contract. A promissory agreement between two or more persons that creates, modifies, or destroys a legal relation. An agreement, upon sufficient consideration, to do or not to do a particular thing.

Curtesy. The estate to which by common law a man is entitled, on the death of his wife, in the lands or tenements of which she was seized in possession in fee simple or in tail during her coverture, provided that they have had lawful issue born alive which might have been capable of inheriting the estate. It is a freehold estate for the term of his natural life.

Desertion. An actual abandonment or breaking off of matrimonial cohabitation, by either of the parties, and a renouncing or refusal of the duties and obligations of the relation, with an intent to abandon or foresake entirely and not to return to or resume matrimonial relations, occurring without legal justification either in the consent or the wrongful conduct of the other party.

Domicile. That place where a man has his true, fixed, and permanent home and principal establishment, and to which whenever he is absent he has intentions of returning.

117

Dower. The provision which the law makes for a widow out of the lands or tenements of her husband, for her support and the nurture of her children.

Ecclesiastical Courts. A system of courts in England, held by authority of the sovereign, and having jurisdiction over matters pertaining to the religion and ritual of the established church.

Equity. The spirit and habit of fairness, justness and right dealing.

Equity (legal). A system of jurisprudence, or branch of remedial justice, administered by certain tribunals, distinct from the common law courts and empowered to decree "equity."

Homestead. The home, the house and the adjoining land where the head of the family dwells; the home farm.

Idiot. A person who has been without understanding from is nativity, and whom the law, therefore, presumes never likely to attain any.

Infant. A person within age, not of age, or not of full age; a person under the age of 21 years; a minor.

Insanity. Unsoundness of mind; madness, mental alienation or derangement. In law, such a want of reason, memory and intelligence as prevents a man from comprehending the nature and consequences of his acts or from distinguishing right from wrong.

Jurisprudence. A power constitutioally conferred upon a judge or magistrate to take cognizance of and determine cases according to the law, and to carry his sentence into execution.

Legislature. The department, assembly or body of men that makes laws for a state or nation.

Presumption (of law). A rule of law that courts and judges shall draw a particular inference from a particular fact, or from particular evidence, unless and until the truth of such inference is disproved.

Residence. Living or dwelling in a certain place, permanently or for a considerable length of time.

Statute. An act of the legislature, the written will of the legislature.

Void. Having no legal force or binding effect.

Voidable. That may be avoided; not absolutely void, or void in itself. These definitions were taken from Black's Law Dictionary.

INDEX